100 ISLAND POEMS
OF GREAT BRITAIN AND IRELAND

Edited by
James Knox Whittet

first published 2005 by IRON Press
5 Marden Terrace
Cullercoats
Northumberland
NE30 4PD
England
tel/fax:+44 (0)191 253 1901
Email: seaboy@freenetname.co.uk
web site: www.ironpress.co.uk

ISBN   0 906228 97 2

printed by
Peterson Printers, Jarrow

FIRST EDITION

IRON Pre

and

IRON Press is

hers

ARTS COUNCIL
ENGLAND

To Ann

FOREWORD

In 1936 the film director, Michael Powell travelled to Britain's remotest inhabited island, Foula, one of the Shetland Isles, to make his film *The Edge of the World*. A year later he described his first sight of Foula:

On a still night in June we neared the little lights of Ham voe at midnight. We were six hours out from Scalloway in a motor-boat. The five peaks of the island lay black against a violet sky. A few fishermen were out under the cliffs. On the port bow the moon shone across the sea and on the starboard the setting sun was shining, and the two glittering paths met and broke in our wake. I have never forgotten it.*

His film was about the death of an even remoter island community: St. Kilda. He used Foula as the setting for the film as its cliffs and seascapes are similarly spectacular. However, almost seventy years later, the island community of Foula still survives against all the odds.

Powell asked the question which many passionate lovers of small islands have asked themselves at some time or other: *Why has an island an irresistible appeal to us all?* His answer was:
...because it is complete. We can see it as a whole. Other places have the same appeal, that we can feel at the first visit, but not in such an intimate, such a concentrated form. A lonely island throws its spell over the traveller as soon as he sets foot on its smallest rock.

To stand on the highest point of a small, remote island is to confront the limits of your world. The sea is all around you. You have all the freedom of a prisoner. A crofter bard on the Hebridean island of Coll said that: *we are a people locked up in the Atlantic*. In the final poem of this anthology, R.S. Thomas writes of *prisoners of the keyless sea* with only *the mind's bread and water* for sustenance.

Having grown up on an island, I know too well those occasional long-ings to escape to the wonderful, vague freedom - wonderful because vague - of the *mainland* where they do things differently and where excitement and fulfilment are to be found. However, many islanders who do leave, return or spend much of their lives longing to return. One's former prison comes to seem a place of release.

There is, of course, a deep sense of comfort and security in being locked up by the sea, surrounded by people you *know to the bone*, in the mem-orable phrase of Iain Crichton Smith. To remove yourself from an island or to have been removed from an island, is to harbour an inexpress-ible sense of loss, a nagging feeling of having had something irrecov-erable taken away from you. To read of the evacuation of islands such as St. Kilda or the Great Blasket Islands is to be reminded of the deep losses we all have experienced in our lives. In the words of Julie O'Callaghan:

Listen, mister, most of us cry sooner or later
over a great Blasket Island of our own.

Those of us who love islands live in a sea of lost islands: the ones we couldn't, or weren't allowed, to settle in or those we couldn't reach. In her autobiography, the lone yachtswoman, Ellen MacArthur writes of her childhood dreams of sailing *to a secret island that had long been forgotten.* But to return to a loved island is too often to find *the bent witches evicted* and replaced by *suave strangers with soft voices* now that *the fairy stories / have gone down to the grave in peace,* as Iain Chrichton Smith writes in *No Return.*

Changed people cannot return to the same island but that knowledge does nothing to assuage the longing to return. *It dies hard, the notion of a just people* writes David Constantine in his poem, *Atlantis.* This long-ing to return to a loved or imagined island is bound up with an even deeper longing to return to a better world and a finer way of living. Albert Einstein expressed a longing which many people must have felt at one time or an other: *How I wish that somewhere there existed an island for those who are wise and of goodwill.* It is difficult not to look at the world and your way of life within it without a faint sense of disgust. We pause at times and look around at our world and long to escape from it and a small, remote island appears as an ideal place of escape. It is, of course, an illusion in that we can't escape from ourselves or entirely from others, but it is a noble illusion.

This longing to live on a self-contained island is partly a longing to be part of a genuine community: a place where one's actions can make a notable difference and where one's presence will be continually acknowledged by those around us. We all want to live in a place where our eventual death will leave a space that won't be hurriedly filled. In a small island, death is a family affair in that each person's death affects, in some way, all of those who remain. Hence the long periods of mourning which were traditionally observed in island communities. Even today, in island newspapers such as the *Stornoway Gazette* in the Outer Hebrides, every islander's death is marked by a short biography of his or her life, however outwardly uneventful that life might have been. The village shop may close on the day of the funeral as island villagers leave routine aside in the face of loss.

In an autobiographical essay entitled *Between Sea and Moor*, Iain Crichton Smith writes of his native island of Lewis:

I love it for its very bleakness, for its very absences… One of my more recent memories is standing on a road on the moor and watching a man and woman cutting peats, bent down into the rain and wind and then suddenly a ray of light, fugitive and serene, falling across them so that for a moment they looked as if they had been framed in a picture without glamour or glory, but rather attesting to the sudden moments of illumination or happiness that come to us out of the grind of existence.

To live on a bare, bleak, often treeless island, is to experience the richness of absences and the fulfilment of emptiness. As Lao Tse reminded us centuries before, the important part of a window isn't the frame but the hole which lets in the light. He went on: *It's the things you don't do, the empty times, which give life value.* As Buddhists tell us, we all have to come back to emptiness in the end. Kay Hathway writes of the Scottish Holy Island where Buddhist nuns and monks spend years in retreat from the world and where: *A woman lifts her arms shoulder high, past / the horizon.* Paradoxically, living on an island can help you transcend the boundaries of place. As the Isle of Wight poet Robin Ford tells us: *Boundaries here are fixed, horizons are limitless.* In the Western world, in particular, perhaps more than ever, many people feel a great desire to retreat from the frantic pace and clutter of the world to a place in which they can reach beyond routine actions and beliefs and recover a sense of wonder at who they are and why they are here. In the words of Etty Hillesum, *sometimes the most important thing in a whole day is the rest we take between two deep breaths.*

Not altogether surprisingly, many poets have felt and succumbed to this irresistible draw of islands. A poet is to a greater or larger extent, one who has not only a life-long love affair with language but a life-long love affair with place. It is wonderfully fitting that we should refer to Hardy country, Brontë country, Clare country and so on. One thinks of Hugh MacDiarmid's nine years 'exile' in the Shetland island of Whalsay, in considerable poverty, but who found:

I was better with the sound of the sea
Than with the voices of men
And in desolate and desert places
I found myself again.

One thinks also of Richard Murphy who lived alone for years on his own *shoulder of rock*, High Island where he listened to petrels:

Quietly as the rustle
Of an arm entering a sleeve,
They slip down to nest
Under altar stone or grave.

Norman MacCaig was haunted by his childhood holidays on the small island of Scalpay, in the Outer Hebrides. When he sets foot on the island after many years' absence, he has *come back from the dead* because: *half my thought and half my blood is Scalpay.*

When R.S. Thomas looks across to *That Place*: Bardsey Island, he express-es that ache so many of us feel of being unable to hold on to that ideal place that we'd once momentarily found and which no subsequent place can match. That place:

that we had found and would spend
the rest of our lives looking for.

Anna Adams and her family returned summer after summer to the tiny Hebridean island of Scarp long after the island had been abandoned by its few remaining inhabitants. Few poets have written so movingly of an island which once was home to generations of men, women and children and where each natural sound, to human ears, still carries a note of loss. An island *may shrug its people off* but even the call of the corncrake hints of a human echo:

It calls and calls, again and then again;
yet is not quite that desolate
repeated call, unanswered, in a house
which people have left forever

Many of the most distinguished British and Irish poets of the twentieth century have been born on islands or have lived significant periods of their lives on islands. This is particularly true of twentieth century Scottish poetry where the names of Edwin Muir, George MacKay Brown, Iain Crichton Smith, Sorley MacLean, Derick Thomson, Hugh MacDiarmid and Norman MacCaig immediately spring to mind. Indeed, far from being peripheral, islands have so often been at the centre of modern poetry, which makes it surprising that there has never previously been an anthology devoted to poems inspired by the islands around the coast of Britain and Ireland.

This anthology is not a gazetteer of islands. I have chosen these hundred poems, by famous and by lesser-known poets, because they have touched me in some way. Poems which have, in the words of Iain Crichton Smith, given voice to those *moments of illumination . . . that come to us out of the grind of existence.* I haven't hesitated to select three or four poems by a little-known poet and one poem from a greatly admired poet since I'm following only the dictates of my own taste. Unlike many anthologies, this is not the mere rounding up of the usual suspects by the lazy and fashion conscious anthologists which clutter the few shelves which most bookshops devote to poetry.

Similarly, I have had no compunction about including three or four poems inspired by a tiny, largely unknown and uninhabited island and one poem inspired by a larger, populous, well-known island. The poems have taken precedence over reputations and over islands. Nonetheless, as you can see at a glance on the maps, I have included poems about islands all around the coast of Scotland, England, Wales, Ulster and Ireland. Here you will discover poems from the tiny island of Scolt Head, *The First Island*, off the coast of Norfolk and journey clockwise around the coast to the Isle of Wight, the Channel Isles, the Scilly Isles, Caldey Island, Bardsey Island, Anglesy, the great Blaskets, the Aran Islands, Rathlin, the Isle of Man, the Inner Hebrides - Islay being the most beautiful and important of these islands! - the Outer Hebrides, including St. Kilda, the Orkney Isles, the Shetland Isles, the islands of the Firth of Forth, Lindisfarne and the Farne Isles and other islands. I have also included poems at the end of the anthology which have not been inspired by any named or any particular island but which convey deep insights about the nature of islands. I hope you will find pleasure and illumination in this poetic voyage or pilgrimage - one thinks of all those early Christian monks, hermits and saints who confronted themselves and God on remote, rain lashed islands all around our coast. We, in the words of Paddy Bushe about the monks of Skellig Michael: *deny, envy / and fear their illumination.*

Sheila Gear who has lived most of her long life on Foula, cultivating her few sparse acres of land, ends her moving book, *Foula: Island West of the Sun* with the recognition that:

Long, long after we are gone from this world, the isle will still be our island. The wind will still roar through the hills, the sea still pound against its cliffs. The isle does not need us, it can stand alone. This is our sorrow and our comfort.

Although it is true that an island can exist without us, it will remain forever altered by those distinctive people who have lived on it. In her book on the abandoned island of Scarp, *Island Chapters*, Anna Adams notes that the most astonishing array of wild flowers grow on land which had been cultivated for generations. It is humans also who possess places through the names which they confer on them. In the Book of Genesis, the animals are brought to Adam for him to name: naming is too important a task to be left to God. It may only be through human naming that any place can truly live. It would be difficult to think of any island more wonderfully named than Foula: Gaada Stack, Soberlie, Hamnafield, the Sneug and so on. It is humans also who create or who discover meanings through the language they use to embody and to shape their experiences. It is humans also who bear witness to the beauty of the world. As the Highland poet, Alasdair Maclean asks of remote hill lochans: *How will they know they are beautiful if I do not tell them so?*

In the following pages, our beautiful islands are given a voice. I hope you will find the quiet moments needed to listen to these island voices.

* Foreword to *The Isle of Foula* by Prof. I.B.S. Holbourn

James Knox Whittet
April 2005

THE ISLAND POEMS

THE FIRST ISLAND

Kevin Crossley-Holland

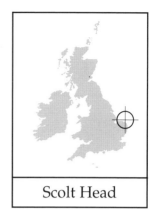

Scolt Head

There it was, the island.

Low-slung sandhills like land-waves, fettered by marram.
One hut, a dark nugget. Across the creeks gleaming like
tin, like obsidian, across the marshes almost rust,
olive, serge, fawn, purpled for a season, the island.

We shoaled on the Staithe, stared out and possessed it;
children who collar half the world with a shout, and
share it in a secret.

Old men sat on a form lodged against the wall.
Of course we did not ask. We knew. They were too old.

There it was, and at times not there. Atmosphere
thickened, earth and air and water became one lung;
we were in a wilderness.

In a coat of changing colours it awaited us. In the
calm seas of our sleep it always loomed, always ahead.
We woke, instantly awake. As if we never had been
tired, and all things were possible.

So the boat came for us. The island stretched out to
us and we took it for granted. And no one asked by
which creeks we had come or could return.

ISLAND

Robin Ford

Isle of Wight

You see I come from here, I can
neither deny it nor expel it from me.
Islands either draw you or repel

hold you tight or tip you from the nest.
Indifference not an option else why stay?
I am caught in a web of hills

lanes and beaches which are frontiers
to all the shores of earth.
These places give themselves to those
who want to know their ways, recoil

from others and I could find no new
way now, but then, not ever
and though I feel for other places too

when sea small - washes over me again
I am like driftwood beached.
Boundaries here are fixed, horizons limitless.

ISLAND

Jane Griffiths

Jersey

Waking, the sounds come first, amorphous
and discordant as
an orchestra tuning.
The mist is banked against the house like snow;
the house is feathered and embedded in it:
it is drifting

(slowly) back to sleep, while somewhere down
below the cloud, day
is finding its voice, piece
by crystalline piece: the five goslings stir,
the gander goes off like a soda siphon
at imagined

alarms and diversions, Vienna
the mare is breezing
in her stall, and beyond
the garden wall, a Range Rover goes by
quivering antennae, with its radio
tuning in to

England, where *it is eight o' clock
on Thursday, the twelfth
of June.* From the window
cropped-off roofs and conifers appear where
France or Guernsey might be on a brighter day.
(It's not clear what

the point of the view is.) Although down
in the valleys this

could almost be mainland,
out on the coast-road improvisation
hangs on in a breeze-block trellis that trebles
as balcony

wine-rack, boot and geranium stand;
in German bunkers
turned fish-farm and in all
the *cotils* where potato leaves flurry
in arrested waterfalls over the roofs
and bantams pass

behind the chimneys: even the land's
doubled up. Out at
the Fisherman's Chapel
in St. Brelade, wall-paintings show coffins
open for the Resurrection (more like boats
or hip-baths than

terra firma coffins) putting out
in a whitewash sea.
Of Christ, just head and limbs
remain: like rocks, like the islanded limbs
of a sleeper. Hands clasped, the buoyant, painted
dead break out of

the stone as if for air, making their
representations
fervently, forever,
while in the main church a placard

commands visitors' prayers, and across the bay
the twice-daily

ferry bluffs its way out through the fog
which may be general
or may be a local
challenge to all comers, like the sign at
the Methodist Chapel that claims (stony-faced)
Truth Is Inside.

ISLANDS

David Constantine

Scillies

1. *Bracken*

There were sheep then, they pastured on the little islands,
We took them there by boat. But the grass has gone
And the fold my father's father built with his bare hands
Here at high water has also gone. One by one
All his fields have gone under the ferns again
And now it is hard for you to see how it was then.

Bitter, unharvested, deeper than children,
The ferns rise from high water over the wall.
The fields drown; the swinging gate is fallen
And ferns break round the posts that stand as tall
As men. But from the spring you climbed this way
After the spilling water-carts on a hot day.

You would not think we had any open ground,
But we did. We called it Plains. There was space
For all the island to be sitting round
Watching the tennis or the cricket. Our playing-place
Has gone the way of the fields and I shouldn't know
Where to look for the pitch and the court now.

Sunk flourishing in depths of bitter green
The little islands are lost to us already.
We watch from boats the rats going hungry between
Waste and waste. Remember for our sakes quickly
Where the sweet water places were and when
And by whom the fields were first rid of their bracken.

Sometimes in summer we made ourselves a bed
Under the ferns, where we should never be found,
And looked up through the lovely green at the sky and said
That we were at the bottom of the sea and drowned.
I believe sometimes we slept, but the afternoon
When we woke again was still no further gone.

We lie on the harbour wall and peering down
Where the wrack heaves and hideous claws feel
After food, we see the clouds that do not drown
In pathless water with all of our things lost but sail
Untouched through the coral and the salt flowers
Through the places of this island that once were ours.

2

At blown cockcrow, hearing the driven sea,
You remember the rattling sash, starlight
Surviving faintly on the looking-glass
And the islands troubled with a ceaseless crying.

Scheria, kind to strangers, wept for her ship
Sunk by God unjustly; for the *Schiller's*
More than three hundred souls there were many in
Two continents weeping; and everywhere

For the sailors of our wars, numberless
Mothers' sons who have rolled in without faces.
Indifferent Hermes conducted them all.
The sea turns and its creatures hunger. Soon

Everything lies under the mercy of day.
The surface flickers with scared pilchards.
Light, above all the light. And the sea comes,
At sunny tide-flow the plucked, the smitten sea

Comes running. The wind then, high-ridden by
One nonchalant gull, batters the opening
Eyes of the sun with water. Far-reaching,
Iridescent, the white surf comes and comes.

Children are playing under a rainbow
On Pool Green; or behind Innisvouls,
Delighted in a rocking boat, they stand
Outstaring the ancient quizziness of seals.

3

Our child when we came looking and calling after her,
And had come through marram and sea-holly to the dunes' crest
When we stood crushing in our fingers plucked samphire
Looking still further and calling and saw her at last

She was remote and small on an almost island
And turned away, at tide-flow, but our fear was less
Of the sea already parting the cord of sand
Than that she was so small and averted from us.

We ran heavily, the white sand sank us in,
But through the neck of the place stole then like bird-stalkers
Over the flat wrack that popped and stank in the sun
Towards her kneeling before big granite chairs

Gently stroking for shells. When she turned and looked up
And showed us wordless in her palm the fissured cowrie
The spiralling white horn of wentletrap
And scallops smaller than her smallest nail then we

With our looks put upon her the fear of death
And the ownership of love. Between our tall shadows
She walked to the safe beach down the snake path
Already sunk over ankles in warm shallows.

Gratefully then the weed rose in the sunny water
And swirled as it liked and flowed and the bright shell
Hoards sparkled before the thrones without her
Who stood between us watching, waiting for tide-fall.

4 *The Drowned*

Flat calm. The ships have gone.
By moonlight and by daylight one by one
Into a different world the drowned men rise
But cannot claw the sleep out of their eyes.
None such can know the bigger light from the less
Nor taste even the salt. Their heaviness
By no means may be leavened. Now they live
As timbers do where shipworms thrive
Only in what they feed. Strange things engross
The little galleries of thought after the loss
Of breath. The white clouds pass, but still
The drowned increase upon the senses till
The moon delivers them. On islands then

Seeing the lovely daylight watchful men
Come down and haul these burdens from the waves
And slowly cart them home and dig them graves.

5

The trees here, though the wind leave off, never unbend.
Likewise when he sat the stick retained
The shape of the sixty years he had limped and leaned.
He would haul from under the bed with the crook-end

His bundle of photographs and the soldier's pay-book,
The usual service medals and a card or two in silk.
The marriage bed was draped to the floor like a catafalque
And he hauled the War from under it. And when he spoke

Of the craters at Ypres he used the pool on Pool Green
As measure, and the island's entanglements of brambles when
He spoke of the wire. He rose, drinking gin,
Massive, straighter than his stick, and boys were shown

At the hoisting of his trouser up the sunless calf
A place that shrank like Lazarus from being raised,
A flesh the iron seemed only lately to have bruised.
And if one, being bidden and not in disbelief,

Put in the hand to prove him right who bet
That he was past hurt there - probing appalled
In that still weeping place the fingers rolled
Wondering between them an angle of iron grit.

For year by year his flesh, till he was dead,
Evicted its shrapnel, as the living ground
Puts out for the Parson or the Schoolmaster to find,
Scouring at leisure, another arrow head.

6 *Spring Tide*

The summer moon was terrible. It beamed
Like Christ on Lazarus. Nobody now,
In daylight, can distinguish what he dreamed
And what he saw, in night-clothes at the window.

It was like All Souls when everything lost
And the smothered dead struggle to rise. Around
Midnight the moon hauled hand over fist
And sheet by sheet the waters were unwound.

But nothing was recovered. Still the sand,
That we saw white and phosphorescent, levels
The slopes and pleasant laps of land
And stops the doorways and the fires and wells.

The curlews cried like springs starting to run.
Then sleep began to fill us and we felt
A weeping rise and flow. Now in the sun
The sea is brimful and our cheeks are wet and salt.

7

Sheer nowhere: the land
Ends, the rocks pile dumbly where they fell,
And hold for any life nearer to ours than lichen
There is none; the useful
Wood of wrecks whitens beyond our reach.

Rain passes, rain on the sea, and sweetens
With all its copious fall
By not one measurable jot the expanse of salt.
Clinging to islands we
Camping with our dead around a sunken plain

Such as we are, late on,
Want above all things passage to one another,
Aid and the sharing of wells
And not to swell our bitterness beyond
The normal allocation of tears.

WILD PAEONY

Brian Biddle

Steepholm

Nowhere but here,
sheltered in limestone clefts
among the crags of Steepholm,
this relic of a monastic past survives.
For centuries it has renewed
its ancient lineage and every year
in crimson robes of state
and with a stamen crown of gold,
asserts a precedence and regal power.

While on the Severn shore
common members of the kingdom
thrive in their workaday way.
Dull glasswort and ordinary fescue
spread their roots in estuary mud.
Only on the contoured sand-banks
a few colonies of anchored marram grass
face the island dome across the river flow
and bow their heads in the prevailing wind.

CALDEY ISLAND

Brother David Hodges

Caldey Island

Battered by wind
and battered by sea,
only a fool would visit,
or make plans,
on an island
where the boats
are all "Weather Permitting".

No good to man
nor beast,
fit only for monks
and for prayer,
when the wind
is gale force
east-south-east.

Only a saint
would visit
in winter.

RAMSEY ISLAND MAKEOVER

Ramsey Island

Kay Hathway

Poorly applied compressed foundation,
streaks of sandstone and red shale-striped
like seaside rock - with a runny nasal extrusion
of larval deposit to accentuate the fault.
Hidden away from pollution, the blush
of pink lichen sits shyly on the cheekbones
of inlaid caves. A living mouth, seal-plump
with lipid tissue and change-coat colour shows
maternal gloss as cows protect their pups.
Thick powder from a thousand thousand
droppings dusts the surface in a cliff-side
coating. Sea-green hair, self-sewn is bound
by royal charter to protect its living crown.
Blue shadow on myriad eyes flying up and
down the cliffs is reflected in the wistful brows
of visitors. Flashes of glimpsed life, fleetingly
recorded, are made up in albums on the mainland.
The island face, unchanged stands proud from the sea.

THAT PLACE

R.S. Thomas

Bardsey Island

I served on a dozen committees;
talked hard, said little, shared the applause
at the end. Picking over
the remains later, we agreed power
was not ours, launched our invective
at others, the anonymous wielders
of such. Life became small, grey,
the smell of interiors. Occasions
on which a clean air entered our nostrils
off swept seas were instances
we sought to recapture. One particular
time after a harsh morning
of rain, the clouds lifted, the wind
fell; there was a resurrection
of nature, and we there to emerge
with it into the anointed
air. I wanted to say to you: "We
will remember this." But tenses
were out of place on that green
island, ringed with the rain's
bow, that we had found and would spend
the rest of our lives looking for.

PRELUDE AND QUESTIONS: ANGLESEY

Alan Pryce-Jones

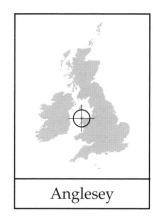

Anglesey

1.

At evening the rocks, the fissures,
the slanted knife-shape like a gull tilting
and the cave becoming an arch and the arch crumbling
hold blue-white light over gravel,
startle like falling of plaster but do not fall:
westward the headlands veil and swell,
the mountain humps above the cooling beeches,
the cars start up, the picnic is dismantled,
a little litter rattles and fills
with the flooding tide, the spine of the conger.

The dogfish egg floats in the darkness.

The dried-out tissue of the sea pink trembles.

2.

Excitement
blesses the objects. Form can give
security. One hides in the attractive
sense of an island. But tonight
by the oil lamp in the parlour
or changing my shoes on the cold linoleum
by the light of a candle, running out the sand,
or turning into the sea-dark at the doorway
vague, warm, the moth in the wind
damp on the privet and fuchsia,
the honeysuckle swung with a tendril
and the ivy clipped to the rock and the heather
wired to its peaty soil,

I shall be ashamed of alliteration
and the obvious delights. I shall be ashamed
of the rootless sensuality that pumps
the blood-red flower and impacts the stone,
for the poem behind the poem is inconsolable.
I shall want to cry with my own voice:
"I have come back. It is after ten years.
How does one learn to live?" And the question,
hidden behind the question, once again
will rise in its unconscionable boyhood
to be the gunman of another twilight.

SALTEE ISLAND

Saltee

Eithne Cavanagh

May has flung wild fistfuls
of bluebells azuring the leeward slope.
On the wilder edge rocks glisten ochre
and palest silver.

Here, gannets glide
past a high sun, their stiff wingspan
filtering light whiter than fine organdie
veiling muscle of their bullet flight.

Invaders on this sanctuary,
we adjust our lenses, greedy to observe.
I almost feel the silky warmth
of gannets' yellow heads.

You stroke my face with a feather
later saved between the pages
of my bird book. I pick a sea campion
to press its papery bloom,

but falter at the sappy stem
of bluebell bowed in a breeze
whispery as the sigh of vespers
just before the evening ferry sails.

SCEILG MONKS

Paddy Bushe

Skellig Michael

They went because the whole
island, its straining peaks,
seemed a constant reaching
in stone towards God.

They coursed its image
through fog and swell
in skin boats, finding
ultimately a landing.

Here was in truth
a hard station, gathering
limpets to sustain nights
praying towards illumination.

And their illumination
whatever it was
on the high rocks
was not anything like

being on safe ground
gathering subjects which move
in their proper time
comfortably into poems.

They would have damned comfort
those high, hard men. Above all
they would have damned
the comfortable soul.

I lift my pen.
All at once, and always,
I deny, envy
and fear their illumination.

THE GREAT BLASKET ISLAND

Julie O'Callaghan

Great Blaskets

Six men born on this island
have come back after twenty-one years.
They climb up the overgrown roads
to their family houses
and come out shaking their heads.
The roofs have fallen in
and birds have nested in the rafters.
All the white-washed rooms
all the nagging and praying
and scolding and giggling
and crying and gossiping
are scattered in the memories of these men.
One says, 'Ten of us, blown to the winds -
some in England, some in America, some in Dublin.
Our whole way of life - extinct.'
He blinks back the tears
and looks across the island
past the ruined houses, the cliffs
and out to the horizon.

Listen, mister, most of us cry sooner or later
over a great Blasket Island of our own.

THE BLASKETS

Peter Fallon

Great Blaskets

A word for every wave
that ebbs and flows,
and wind that blows.

Every day's *memento
mori.*
Everybody has a story.

LOVERS ON ARAN

Seamus Heaney

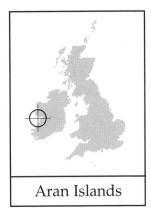

Aran Islands

The timeless waves, bright, sifting, broken glass,
Came dazzling around, into the rocks,
Came glinting, sifting from the Americas

To possess Aran. Or did Aran rush
To throw wide arms of rock around a tide
That yielded with an ebb, with a soft crash?

Did sea define the land or land the sea?
Each drew new meaning from the waves' collision.
Sea broke on land to full identity.

MORNING WALK, SEPTEMBER 12th, 2001

Gerard Hanberry

Aran Islands

Here is the blue silence of
a western headland,
the bay sparkling silver,
the Burren sloping to Black Head,
and out there on the edge, Aran,
shimmering like three half-formed stanzas
or islands you can see
only if you believe.

But a gull swoops past,
shocking in its siver wing-spread,
its tilt, a fireball conjured.
Now all the wild-eyed birds
are shrieking, wheeling,
plunging headlong through
the incandescent sky.

LEAVING INISHMORE

Michael Longley

Inishmore

Rain and sunlight and the boat between them
Shifted whole hillsides through the afternoon -
Quiet variations on an urgent theme
Reminding me now that we left too soon
The island awash in wave and anthem.

Miles from the brimming enclave of the bay
I hear again the Atlantic's voices,
The gulls above us as we pulled away -
So munificent their final noises
These are the broadcasts from our holiday.

Oh, the crooked walkers on that tilting floor!
And the girls singing on the upper deck
Whose hair took the light like a downpour -
Interim nor change of scene shall shipwreck
Those folk on the move between shore and shore.

Summer and solstice as the seasons turn
Anchor our boat in a perfect standstill,
The harbour wall of Inishmore astern
Where the Atlantic waters overspill -
I shall name this the point of no return

Lest that excursion out of light and heat
Take on a January idiom -
Our ocean icebound when the year is hurt,
Wintertime past cure - the curriculum
Vitae of sailors and the sick at heart.

ISLANDER

Michael O'Siadhial

Inishmaan

A palm spread on the brow or tipping the hands
Would somehow help to both remember and forget,
Clay on clay, our old rituals of acceptance.

From the Jersey shore New York haloed a horizon
That night word came. It might have been Galway's
Shimmering skyline as the steamer left Inishmaan

Thirty years ago on his first visit to that city;
Reluctant pioneer, lover of the way things were,
Last unwilling convert to slates and electricity.

Oceans apart, my memory strives to fix its image.
'A man without help must depend on himself.'
He crouches and pokes his potato-sets in a ridge.

There was such delight, a sweated awkward dignity
Prides in his skills. And that half-smirk half-smile:
'So that's the way it's done. And now don't you see?'

For him no cities, his Promised Land an inheritance,
A stewardship between the gone and the yet unborn.
Always he seems to touch his earth with reverence.

All agog I'm standing there and once more a son
Learning to spread seaweed, how to mould the earth.
A man with a gift and where will he pass it on?

At eighty it's Dublin for radium. Still stubborn,
Alarmed at that lump, he defers a final pilgrimage.
'If I go now, sure I know that I'll never return.'

A thread of shoreline vanishes in the sleepless glow.
Lean radiance of dreams. Skid Row. Babbling towers.
Insomniac Camelot. Huge city of get-up-and-go.

I'm trying to imagine the podgy cold of his forehead.
He's kneeling to palm down a fistful of damp clay.
Quick stab of his dibble, the set darkens in its bed.

THE OLD WOMAN'S REEL

Valerie Gillies

Aran Islands

She is at the small deep window
looking through and out:
the Aran islands, rock and seawater,
lie all about.
A face strong in poverty's hauteur
is hers, then and now.

Being a young woman in Flaherty's film
'Man of Aran',
she nearly drowned in the undertow
by the boat where she ran.
He kept on filming even though
he thought her dead on the rockrim.

A body plaited by water twine
they carried ashore:
partnered in the ocean's set dance
by two men or more.
The sea had had its chance
to peel her off by the shoreline.

Now in her great old age
toothless and tough,
the island music still delights her:
one dance is not enough.
The tunes of a people poor and cut off there
have a special power to engage.

Drawn upright, her stiff bones
already dancing,
she spins, not on one foot
but on her stick, tap-balancing.
While to one side like a pliant offshoot
a little girl mimics her, unbeknown.

HIGH ISLAND

Richard Murphy

High Island

A shoulder of rock
Sticks high up out of the sea,
A fisherman's mark
For lobster and blue-shark.

Fissile and stark
The crust is flaking off,
Seal-rock, gull-rock,
Cove and cliff.

Dark mounds of mica schist,
A lake, mill and chapel,
Roofless, one gable smashed,
Lie ringed with rubble.

An older calm,
The kiss of rock and grass,
Pink thrift and white sea-campion,
Flowers in the dead place.

Day keeps lit a flare
Round the north pole all night.
Like brushing long wavy hair
Petrels quiver in flight.

Quietly as the rustle
Of an arm entering a sleeve,
They slip down to nest
Under altar stone or grave.

Round the wrecked laura
Needles flicker
Tacking air, quicker and quicker
To rock, sea and star.

WALKING ON SUNDAY

Richard Murphy

Omey Island

Walking on Sunday into Omey Island
　When the tide had fallen slack,
I crossed a spit óf wet ribbed sand
　With a cold breeze at my back.

Two sheepdogs nosed me at a stile,
　Boys chevied on the green,
A woman came out of a house to smile
　And tell me she had seen

Men digging down at St. Fechin's church,
　Buried in sand for centuries
Up to its pink stone gable top, a perch
　For choughs and seapies.

I found a dimple scalloped from a dune,
　A landing-slip for coracles,
Two graveyards - one for women, one for men -
　Odorous of miracles:

And twelve parishioners probing a soft floor
　To find what solid shape there was
Under shell-drift; seeking window, door;
　And measuring the house.

48

Blood was returning dimly to the face
  Of the chancel they'd uncovered,
Granite skin that rain would kiss
  Until the body flowered.

I heard the spades clang with a shock
  Inaugurating spring:
Fechin used plug and feather to split rock
  And poised the stone to sing.

He tuned cacophony to make
  Harmony in this choir:
The ocean gorged on it, he died of plague,
  And hawks nested there.

TONY WHITE AT INISHBOFIN

Richard Murphy

1959

Inishbofin

With a lobster pot for a chair
And a fishbox for a table
He'd sacrificed a plausible career
On the London stage to live near
The sea in a bare room
Far from home
To become on the lips of islanders a fable.

In an old pair of black jeans
Threadbare though tautly darned
By himself needling with a woman's patience
Buckled in a looted Hun's
Eagle and swastika belt
Disguised he felt
Reborn as a fisherman whose craft he learned.

From an off-white Aran sweater
Knit by his neighbour's wife
His dark face opened like a long love-letter
That makes a forlorn reader
Revive with a gust of hope
While he moused rope
For crayfish traps with a horn gutting knife.

Through small panes of cobwebbed glass
Across a limewashed stone sill
He hauled in shoals of riffled sun to please
Only a few friends like us
Because it was his style
To play as well
Carrying a creel on his back or Coriolanus.

INISHBOFIN SHEEP SHEARING

Eithne Cavanagh

Inishbofin

'Three sheep a day
is enough for a woman'
half-moon metal
gleaming in your hand.

Two days ago
you almost lost your man,
a coronary while fishing.
Now your keen eye regards
three ewes, legs trussed,
twitching on green plastic.

We try to help.
Eyeball to eyeball with a sheep
for the first time,
our city hands
feel rough ridges of horn
and delicacy of ankle,
holding her steady
for your expert cut.

Free at last, bald, vulnerable,
she stumbles on dainty hooves
looking prehistoric.
Her twin lambs bleat, hesitate
then rush for milk.

Anointed with oily fleece
we prepare to handle
two more ewes,
your quota for today.

THE ACHILL WOMAN

Eavan Boland

Achill Island

She came up the hill carrying water.
She wore a half-buttoned, wool cardigan,
a tea-towel round her waist.

She pushed the hair out of her eyes with
her free hand and put the bucket down.

The zinc-music of the handle on the rim
tuned the evening. An Easter moon rose.
In the next-door field a stream was
a fluid sunset; and then, stars.

I remember the cold rosiness of her hands.
She bent down and blew on them like broth.
And round her waist, on a white background,
in coarse, woven letters, the words 'glass cloth'.

And she was nearly finished for the day.
And I was all talk, raw from college -
weekending at a friend's cottage
with one suitcase and the set text
of the Court poets of the Silver Age.

We stayed putting down time until
the evening turned cold without warning.
She said goodnight and started down the hill.

The grass changed from lavender to black.
The trees turned back to cold outlines.
You could taste frost

but nothing now can change the way I went
indoors, chilled by the wind

and made a fire
and took down my book
and opened it and failed to comprehend

the harmonies of servitude,
the grace music gives to flattery
and language borrows from ambition -

and how I fell asleep
oblivious to

the planets clouding over in the skies,
the slow decline of the spring moon,
the songs crying out their ironies.

TORY ISLAND IMAGES

Eithne Cavanagh

Tory Island

1   *Artist's Hut*

In the unbelievably blue sphere
of sea and sky she peels an orange

and separates the segments.
Juice splashes the saffron-lichened rocks.

On tiptoe at the artist's hut
she sees a moth trapped behind grimy glass,

a tub of pollyfilla, empty coat hangers
pillows, their ticking all torn.

Linseed oil, paintbrushes stiff with disuse
seem to wait for his ghost

to sweep across canvas
capture the vastness, release the moth.

2   *Legends*

Etching the skyline Errigal, Muckish
are robed in bleached denim haze.

Her world is fragrant with ozone and pollen
faded seapinks flutter papery shells.

Chough, cormorants and gulls wheel
by crags unchanged since one-eyed Balor

imprisoned his daughter for daring to love,
or since Columcille blessed a handful of clay.

She finishes her orange, zest scenting the blue
with hints of Morocco, 'African Mariners',

pirates of legend and poem.
She dreams ships laden with gold, spices and silk.

A moth wings past her head,
like a spirit following flight to infinity.

3   *The Ceili*

At midnight or so the music starts.
Patsy Dan's accordion sets toes a-twitching.

The *Waves of Tory* and the *Stack of Barley*
undulate around the hall.

A sixteen-hand reel gains momentum,
its rhythms spiralling into time.

The human whirligig spins faster, faster
while a bodhran speeds up the beat.

Music spilling out over her head,
she dances towards the lighthouse beam

to the fringe of the world where the artist's hut
stands black and angled against the moon.

The English painter, Derek Hill encouraged the native painters on the island.

RATHLIN

Derek Mahon

Rathlin

A long time since the last scream cut short -
Then an unnatural silence; and then
A natural silence, slowly broken
By the shearwater, by the sporadic
Conversation of crickets, the bleak
Reminder of a metaphysical wind.
Ages of this, till the report
Of an outboard motor at the pier
Shatters the dream-time and we land
As if we were the first visitors here.

The whole island a sanctuary where amazed
Oneiric species whistle and chatter,
Evacuating rock-face and cliff-top.
Cerulean distance, an oceanic haze -
Nothing but sea-smoke to the ice-cap
And the odd somnolent freighter.
Bombs doze in the housing estates
But here they are through with history -
Custodians of a lone light which repeats
One simple statement to the turbulent sea.

A long time since the unspeakable violence -
Since Somhairle Buí, powerless on the mainland,
Heard the screams of the Rathlin women
Borne to him, seconds later, upon the wind.
Only the cry of the shearwater
And the roar of the outboard motor
Disturb the singular peace. Spray-blind,
We leave here the infancy of the race,
Unsure among the pitching surfaces
Whether the future lies before us or behind.

FROM WALNEY ISLAND

Norman Nicholson

Walney Island

This shore looks back to England: two hundred yards
Of tide, and the boats fratching on their leashes
Like dogs that sniff a stranger. An oily fog
Smudges the mud-mark till the screes of slag
Seem floating on the water. Smoke and fog
Wash over crane and derrick, and chimneystacks
Ripple and ruck in the suck and swim of the air
Like fossil trunks of trees in a drowned forest.
Away in the docks the unlaunched hulls of ships
Seem sunk already, lying on the swash bed
With barnacles and algae.
               The sea
Flows up the channel, and the insulated eye,
Picking and prodding among old boots and cobbles,
Selects and builds a private landscape - fancy,
Finned like a fish, flashes about an abstract
Underwater world of shapes and shadows,
Where men are only movement, where fire and furnace
Are only highlights, lines and angles. Forms
Lose their function, names soak off the labels,
And upside-down is rightways, while the eye,
Playing at poet with a box of colours,
Daubs its pleasures across the sky.

                          The tide
Turns and slides back, and banks of mud
Heave up like waking sleepers pushing the sheets aside;
And, linking shore to shore, emerges
A dripping rib of concrete, half bridge, half causeway,
With neither curb nor handrail,
A foot above the water. Bare toes or hobnails,
Gripping among the slime and seaweed, find
A short cut to the cockles or to work.
                            And like a stone
Thrown through a window pane, the path
Smashes the panorama, pricking the pattern, bringing back
A human meaning to the scene. Shadows
Are walls again, angles revert to roofs,
And roofs and walls relate themselves to men.
The hunger of a hundred thousand lives
Aches into brick and iron, the pain

Of generations in continual childbirth
Throbs through the squirming smoke, and love and need
Run molten into the cold moulds of time.

THE SOUND OF MORNING

Isle of Man

Robert Cortean Carswell

The mist of dawn blew away before the light breeze.
The curtain was being opened to let in
the fresh, new day. The rising of the sun.
A chink of light won its way into the room
through a little gap, going from dust to dust.
The ray caught the spider's web
that was connecting the room's ceiling to the wall.
Suddenly, an alarm clock raised its clarion,
as it threw its noise throughout the house,
in each corner,
but alas, the clock lost heart.
There was not a hand to turn it off,
there was not a voice to swear with hatred at it.
The summons faded away without answer.
The house was as quiet and still as though it was underground.

Translated from Manx by the Author

AN ARRAN DEATH

Edwin Morgan

Arran

When the canon lay dying on the island
in his long strength at ninety-four
and his closest friend came to visit him
after many years, and sat by his head
in the stormbound cottage, and talked,
the old man gazed at him
while rain beat on the sea
patiently, said at last,
I want to thank you for everything you've done -
especially the crucifixion.

The shutters banged. He lay staring at his friend.

ISLE OF ARRAN

Alastair Reid

Arran

Where no-one was was where my world was stilled
into hills that hung behind the lasting water,
a quiet quilt of heather where bees slept,
and a single slow bird in circles winding
round the axis of my head.

Any wind being only my breath, the weather
stopped, and a woollen cloud smothered the sun.
Rust and a mist hung over the clock of the day.
A mountain dreamed in the light of the dark
and marsh mallows were yellow for ever.

Still as a fish in the secret loch alone
I was held in the water where my feet found ground
and the air where my head ended,
all thought a prisoner of the still sense -
till a butterfly drunkenly began the world.

HOLY ISLAND

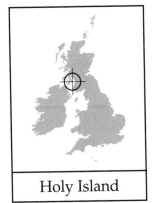

Holy Island

Kay Hathway

A westerly wind whispers through sea grass,
each blade bends in continuous cadence.
A woman lifts her arms shoulder high, past
the horizon, angles her foot and leans
forward, turning her right hand to ramparts
from where guillemots dive for fish and spread
selvedged wings underwater to dart and
seize in sequence. The woman's inner strength
is yin, yang for gentleness of movement,
her limbs the extension of swallowed depth
for solitude seekers. The attendant
animation, a rhythmic form of self.
Bird and woman pursue related goals
to fuel the belly and to feed the soul.

(Holy Island has recently been purchased by Buddhists
and T'ai Chi, a marshall art form, is practised)

GIGHA

W.S. Graham

Gigha

That firewood pale with salt and burning green
Outfloats its men who waved with a sound of drowning
Their saltcut hands over mazes of this rough bay.

Quietly this morning beside the subsided herds
Of water I walk. The children wade through the shallows.
The sun with long legs wades into the sea.

ISLAND POEMS

Iain Crichton Smith

Islay

(1)
Kilnave Churchyard, Islay

In this calm place the graves are very old,
the writing almost illegible. Many men
are lying here with their wives and children,
families reconciled in stone
under the earth's green billows. As we read
in the loud sound of the Atlantic
a lark flies straight up singing. There's a grave
newly open with a spade inside it.
A large hare leaps from behind a stone
and dashes crazily from us. The sky holds
us and the dead, our flesh and the old stones,
some of which are bare of writing.
Imagine how in winter the wind howls
round the unwritten stone, unglamorous, poor.
But now the world is totally calm.
The Atlantic glitters gaily. My hand is warm
leaning on this stone. My shirt is rippling.
The hare has gone to ground, the lark is singing.
The dead knew this joy, they are part of this joy now.

(2)
On the Beach, Islay

This shore is strewn with bones, bottles of Parazone
cast from the ships, strange shells and stony mines,
boxes of wood, old teeth, and rotting shoes.

It is a book we'd read if we could read
on this wide morning full of glittering blue
both of the sea and sky and of your dress.

The seagull plucked monotonously to the beak,
these half burned oranges, this pool of sour brine,
they look hopelessly, asking what they mean.

We meet two tourists walking along the sand
as on a white street bare of traffic,
we say Good Morning quietly as we pass.

The open clams are slowly turning to powder.
The yellow seaweed's drifting. There's the smell
pungent and powerful of the cleansing brine.

A seagull squints at us from the sea's edge.
A sheep grazes above us. There's a ship
moving across the horizon, very slow.

Everything is food. Love do not look at me.
We came out of the sea, we go into the land.
Love, look at me now. It is all sparkling.

(3)
An Islander Speaks

I was born in this village seventy years ago.
I have ploughed my land, I have harvested.
I know everyone to the bone, they know me.
We are, to each other, open doorways.

I was married to a village girl.
I have ploughed my land, I have harvested.
Her motions were of the sea, now of the land.
Her grave flesh entrances me more each day.

(4)

Let us lie here and sleep
in the noise of the Atlantic,
our coats arranged below us.

And, dozing, hear the hum
of the sea in our bones.
We came from the oceans

to this place. Millions of years
it took us. Isn't it puzzling,
isn't it an enigma of the sea,

to have come together as salmon to salmon
imperfectly perfected
for our long meeting?

(5)

You say, "I am sad at leaving the island."
The ship rises and falls
away from, towards the gulls.
We sink into a sleep which heals
us of the island's distance
from the mainland's rushed nerves.
When later we waken
it'll be different again
we shall be ready to enter
by that harsher newer door.

MOVING WITH THE TIMES

James Knox Whittet

Islay

He sat in the back row of the classroom
drawing the faces of clocks, his blunted
pencil rounding a smudged penny; the drum
of rain sounding on the corrugated
roof: dates eroding at his fingertips.
In each separate circle, both short hands
would reach unsteadily to numbers scrawled
around the frayed circumference, his lips
pursed: engrossed in motions of time while strands
of weak sunlight, when the rain had ceased, sprawled

across distempered walls where maps, stained pink,
were stretched out between two pins. He was born
with a fault, his brain unable to link
his thoughts: a jigsaw with the pieces too worn
to fit. He worked on the croft, his mother,
widowed, took in men to stretch her income.
When moving, woodwormed floorboards had settled
down for the night and the moon formed rivers
of light across faded linoleum
flowers, he'd listen as trapped sheep wrestled

with fences, making tightened barbed wires strum.
Mornings, in his black wellies, overturned
and greying, he'd shove barrowloads of dung
beneath wet, arched trees; on the loch, swans preened
their dark brood; above his bent head, white -fronted
geese arrowed for the ocean and left pale
reflections of themselves on stilled water.
A tractor brought mounds of clay into bleached
lines in fields where worms were upturned to veils
of gulls. In misted light, buzzards loitered

in moist gulfs of air. He died an old man
of twenty-seven, leaving behind heaps
of nameless jotters, their pages of worn
circles, moving with the times. Those keepsakes
his mother burnt in a tidying fit
with ripped empty, yellow bags of hen feed:
dog-eared pages curled in flames extended
by stray breezes making flecks of ash flit
and rise and drawn, unsteady hands recede
as singed circumferences contracted.

ISLAND WEDDING

James Knox Whittet

Islay

It is an Islay evening and the winds
from the Atlantic have grown still
and the September sun is letting
go, reluctantly, its last clasp of the hills.

Beneath the slopes of divided fields,
the coupled dead lie hollowed in order
behind dry stoned walls, their long sleep
lulled by the black cattle's lowing.

A path leads through woods to the church,
where elm branches are shaken by the glistening
wings of rooks who call out and call
out to each other with deep voices,

crossing and re-crossing the flowered
gravel with their shadowed flight paths
like those intricate, unbroken
lines chiselled on Kildalton Cross.

Sunlight melts into the fires of sunset
and is reduced to ashes of dusk, then candles
flame from within, making stained figures on
glass dance their way into the darkness.

When the vows have been vowed and
the hymns have been sung and the toasts
all consumed, we make our way past Loch Indaal
on whose moon enamelled surface, two mute

swans fold their separate wings
into a single, moving image of themselves
with Port Charlotte and Bruichladdich
reaching out glowing fingers to touch

Bowmore, where men stand still beneath lamps
at corners, haloed by light pools like Rembrandt's
nightwatchmen: we steal past them, gathering
as we go, ringed handfuls of low-slung stars.

THE FISHERMAN *(Lifting the Creels)*

Colonsay

Donald A MacNeill

Light is my step as I head for the boat;
the skylark is happily welcoming the day.
If I can get under way at the height of full tide,
a pull in the current will get her stern moving.

Many a sight do I spy while at sea:
small seals like sheep on the rocks, fast asleep;
a black cormorant - the great fisherman - searching the waves,
and the kittiwake putting me in mind of my youth.

How often, as a boy, would I climb the cliff paths,
searching for her eggs, my heart pounding,
my toes in a crevice and holding on by my fingernails,
the screaming of seagulls filling my ears.

A faithful little black guillemot is always close by me,
carefully, diligently gathering her food.
Like a falling star, sparkling like gold,
with a splash on the water the great gannet comes.

In *Caolas na Caillich* the current will be the way I like it,
Dubh Hirteach in sight, standing out to the west.
If I can line up the *Dubh-sgeir* on the cairn of *Beinn Riabhach*,
I shall not be left wanting when I pull up a creel.

Though the skies may be darkened by scudding clouds,
and spindrift from the wavetops wetting the sail,
I shall have no worries, so long as the ropes hold;
listening to their music is like a choir in my ears.

Translated from Gaelic by Alistair Scouller

AT THE FIRTH OF LORNE

Iain Crichton Smith

Mull, Kerrera, Tiree

In the cold orange light we stared across
to Mull and Kerrera and far Tiree.
A setting sun emblazoned your bright knee
to a brilliant gold to match your hair's gold poise.

Nothing had changed: the world was as it was
a million years ago. The slaty stone
slept in its tinged and aboriginal iron.
The sky might flower a little, and the grass

perpetuate its sleep. But from the sea
the bare black islands rose, beyond the few
uneasy witticisms we let pursue
their desolate silences. There was no tree

nor other witness to the looks we gave
each other there, inhuman as if tolled
by some huge bell of iron and of gold,
I no great Adam and you no bright Eve.

THE BUZZARD

Myles Campbell

Mull, Kerrera, Tiree

Mull of the spacious moors
and the deserted towns;
and buzzard wakes.
Listening to the oral tradition of the wind.

Translated from Gaelic by the Author

IONA DANCE

Iona

Alix Brown

Somehow the air seems to dance differently here,
executing a perfect back-flip into the arms of the short-cropped hillsides,
gliding in sequinned splendour and perfect three-four time
across the machair,
juggling with rooks and tossing them ragged,
into the raw wind,
swaying, arms entwined, with the green flags
and the surprised white daisies,
somersaulting spectacularly over the cotton grass,
jitterbugging with the spray and
jiving with the spinning sun-specks
over the water,
tapping in time with the tip-tapping pebbles
as they partner the dinner-jacketed oyster-catchers,
line dancing on the telephone wires
to the hum of other people's messages,
smooching in a long, last waltz with the silver sands . . .
somehow, here, the air just dances.

THE STONES OF
IONA AND COLUMBA

George Bruce

Iona

They define themselves rarely
in the walls of the abbey, each
inviting attention as it shapes
in the mind, pink, grey, blue.

So through the glass of sea
on the white bed each stone,
insisting on its difference, presents
itself for the first time,

surprising us with the shock of light
and with the knowledge that it,
like God, has never been seen,
but with love a little known.

The sea pitches. The boat is thrown
on the stony beach. The cliffs echo.
A thousand years ago or more he
picked up green translucent pebbles.

Still they are strange to us. It is enough
the stones stay.

ARGYLE'S RETURN TO THE HOLY ISLAND

Thomas Lynch

Iona

After the dream of the churchdove and the tongues,
Argyle contemplated pilgrimage
to that blessed island in the Hebrides
from which his ancient lineage had sprung
from the sainted loinage of Columbans,
whose couplings with the island women left
a legacy of zealotry, God-hunger,
genius and the occasional idiot
that worked its way down blighted centuries
of monks and anchorites and sin-eaters -
a race of men much gifted with their mouths
for giving out with prayers and poetry
or, like Argyle, for the eating of
sinful excess, shortfalls, mediocrities,
such as would set most lesser men to vomiting.
With neither mule nor map, Argyle walked
aimlessly throughout the western places
until he came to water which he crossed
from island to smaller island praising
the fierce weather, the full moon, the faithful boatman.
What makes this aching in the soul? he thought
for distant islands where the silence hordes
the voices of our dead among the stones?
And though no answer was forthcoming, he went forth.

NIGHT LANDING CANNA

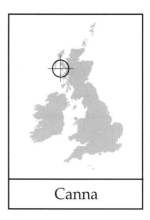

Canna

Angela Blacklock-Brown

We tie up on shore and
time-slip to a distant age.
Moon dancing on water
spotlight's phosphorescence.
We cup our hands
and cull the harvest.
Plankton dart through fingers,
split vision to mosaics.
We rise, watch waves
lap-dissolve on land,
rhythms marking time
ripple the sand.

RETURN TO CANNA

Kathleen Raine

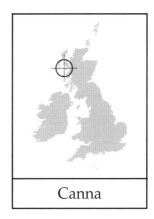

Canna

Long distances of land and sea
Have brought me once more to the gate
Sheltered by its gale-bent trees,
The escalonia avenue,
As if an old beginning were
With each return rehearsed anew
And I had travelled back through time
Towards the welcome of this house.

And in the drawing-room, where all
Is as it was, or little changed,
As in a dream some small detail
Betrays, and warns us, when we wake
That we in sleep had not returned
In truth to the remembered place,
Only almost this now seems then,
The self I am the self I was.

Or as the pictures on a screen
That make a story seem to run
Continuous, one unbroken theme,
Are images that may be seen
Each a still photograph, so here
The abiding present of the past
So clear, I half expect to see
Again the friend who brought me here.

On that cloudless day in spring
So many stormy years ago
When first I sailed into this bay,
Was all my future course laid down,
Was I already what I am
And all the evil I have done
Enfolded in my happy heart?
I called it love, that seed of harm.

SABBATH

Stewart Conn

Skye

Overnight the wind shifts
from south-west to north-east:
we are into a new season.
The Tourist Board seals
sunning themselves in Loch Slapin
have taken the money and run.

Those mountains that looked as if
you could lean out and touch them
have come clean: they were
contours in the imagination.
The blueness of the other side
might have been invented.

And it's the sabbath. Well, serve
it right - all week the Blackface
have been looking down their noses
like Wee Frees, at a spritely pigeon
with a birch-twig in its beak
masquerading as a dove of peace.

GAELIC

Rody Gorman

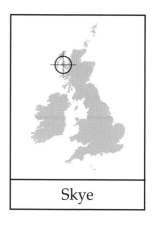

Skye

Someone's wife died in the village
With loads of Gaelic
Unbeknownst to herself:

It was no great surprise
The day of her funeral
That there wasn't a sound on our lips
But the apposite silence
Suiting her speech forever.

A DREAM OF
THE DALAI LAMA ON SKYE

Kathleen Jamie

Skye, Canna, Soay

A summer wind blows the horn of Glen Brittle.
It's a hard walk, Black Cuillin
to his left hand; asks
the midsummer moon
setting over Canna, *what metaphors*
does the market whisper?
If the hills changed shape,
                    who would tell me?
She shines on ditches choked
with yellow iris: butter-lamps
in a temple corner; a snail-shell
in his moonlit palm:
the golden dimple of an icon's smile.
                    He smiles too, notes
the private union of burn and sea,
as one by one, laverocks rise,
irises open. When no one's watching,
he jumps lightly onto Soay
and airborne seeds
of saxifrage, settled
                    on the barren Cuillin
waken into countless tiny stars.

HALLAIG

Sorley MacLean

Raasay

'Time, the deer, is in the wood of Hallaig'

The window is nailed and boarded
through which I saw the West
and my love is at the Burn of Hallaig,
a birch tree, and she has always been

between Inver and Milk Hollow,
here and there about Baile-chuirn:
she is a birch, a hazel,
a straight, slender young rowan.

In Screapadal of my people
where Norman and Big Hector were,
their daughters and their sons are a wood
going up beside the stream.

Proud tonight the pine cocks
crowing on the top of Cnoc an Ra,
straight their backs in the moonlight -
they are not the wood I love.

I will wait for the birch wood
until it comes up by the cairn,
until the whole ridge from Beinn na Lice
will be under its shade.

If it does not, I will go down to Hallaig,
to the Sabbath of the dead,
where the people are frequenting,
every single generation gone.

They are still in Hallaig,
MacLeans and MacLeods,
all who were there in the time of Mac Gille Chaluim
the dead have been seen alive.

The men lying on the green
at the end of every house that was,
the girls a wood of birches,
straight their backs, bent their heads.

Between the Leac and Fearns
the road is under mild moss
and the girls in silent bands
go to Clachan as in the beginning,

and return from Clachan,
from Suisnish and the land of the living;
each one young and light-stepping,
without the heartbreak of the tale.

From the Burn of Fearns to the raised beach
that is clear in the mystery of the hills,
there is only the congregation of the girls
keeping up the endless walk,

coming back to Hallaig in the evening,
in the dumb living twilight,
filling the steep slopes,
their laughter a mist in my ears,

and their beauty a film on my heart
before the dimness comes on the kyles,
and when the sun goes down behind Dun Cana
a vehement bullet will come from the gun of Love;

and will strike the deer that goes dizzily,
sniffing at the grass-grown ruined homes;
his eye will freeze in the wood,
his blood will not be traced while I live.

Translated from Gaelic by the Author

SEAMAN, 1941

Molly Holden

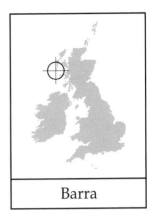

Barra

This was not to be expected.

Waves, wind, and tide brought him again
to Barra. Clinging to driftwood many hours
the night before, he had not recognised
the current far offshore his own nor
known he drifted home. He gave up, anyway,
some time before the smell of land had reached out
or dawn outlined the morning gulls.

                    They found him
on the white sand southward of the ness,
not long enough in the sea to be
disfigured, cheek sideways as in sleep,
old men who had fished with his father
and grandfather and knew him at once,
before they even turned him on his back, by the set
of the dead shoulders, and were shocked.

This was not to be expected.

His mother, with hot eyes, preparing the parlour
for his corpse, would have preferred, she thought,
to have been told by telegram rather
than so to know that convoy, ship and son
had only been a hundred miles north-west
of home when the torpedoes struck.
She could have gone on thinking that
he'd had no chance; but to die offshore,
in Hebridean tides, as if he'd stayed
a fisherman for life and never gone to war
was not to be expected.

PERFECT

Hugh MacDiarmid

On the Western Seaboard of South Uist

I found a pigeon's skull on the machair,
All the bones pure white and dry, and chalky,
But perfect,
Without a crack or a flaw anywhere.

At the back, rising out of the beak,
Were twin domes like bubbles of thin bone,
Almost transparent, where the brain had been
That fixed the tilt of the wings.

NORTH UIST

Stewart Conn

North Uist

I

My new waders are like far-off dogs, whining.
My shoulder-strap could be a wheatear
turning a corner. The wind, through the cleat
of my landing-net, makes the squeaking
of many mice busying themselves under cover.
On his ledge overlooking the loch
the buzzard that is too big for a buzzard
eyes everything stonily, then takes his pick.

II

Uist, a smashed mirror.
I holiday here, to gather
strengths for the winter.
So I fire my peats, gut
trout, rub cold hands together:
reassured that when December
does come, I shall be far
from here. Like all city dwellers.

III

I try to locate a tiny ratchet
at my right ear, an insomniac
cheese-grater somewhere beyond my toes.
The place is hoaching with mice. They are in
for the winter. Every so often
we have an eyeball to eyeball confrontation.
One way to dispose of them is to fire
the thatch. A costly operation.

IV

Three days I have trudged
after a pair of eagles; sighting them
occasionally, overhead or on fence-stakes,
surveying their land. This evening,
probing gobbets of fur, disgorged bone,
I am perceived by a hind who stands
sniffing, then bounds over the wire
and effortlessly away.

V

Striding back from the Co-op, I clutch
sodden groceries in a plastic bag
one handle of which is sprung.
Proud of the buffeting
I'm taking, I feel I belong:
till I meet a chained mongrel,
yap-yapping; and an old woman
who slurches past, head down.

VI

The sky consists of strips
of blue, like a holiday postcard.
I sit writing, like a man writing
a holiday postcard. The strips
turn to steel, to smoky grey.
The tide recedes, and recedes,
all the way to Vallay. Meanwhile
the multitudinous sandworms turn and turn.

VII

If, as the pundits say,
a new Ice Age does
come, well I suppose Uist
will be as ready as most.
The skuas sharp as razors;
the lochans, crystal.
And in the long chambers,
the War Lords are sleeping still.

BELOW THE CLISHAM, ISLE OF HARRIS: AFTER MANY YEARS

Norman MacCaig

Harris

On the mountain pass to Maraig
I met an old woman
darker but only just
than the bad weather we were in.

She was leading a cow by a rope
all the way round the mountain
to Tarbert.

She spoke to me in a misty voice,
glad to rest, glad to exercise
her crippled, beautiful English.

Then they trudged on, tiny
in a murky space
between the cloud of the Clisham
and a tumbledown burn.

And I suddenly was back home again
as though she were her people's history
and I one of her descendants.

RETURN TO SCALPAY

Norman MacCaig

Scalpay

The ferry wades across the kyle. I drive
The car ashore
On to a trim tarred road. A car on Scalpay?
Yes, and a road where never was one before.
The ferrymen's Gaelic wonders who I am
(Not knowing I know it), this man back from the dead,
Who takes the blue-black road (no traffic jam)
From by Craig Lexie over to Bay Head.

A man bows in the North wind, shaping up
His lazybeds,
And through the salt air vagrant peat smells waver
From houses where no house should be. The sheds
At the curing station have been newly tarred.
Aunt Julia's house has vanished. The Red Well
Has been bulldozed away. But sharp and hard
The church still stands, barring the road to Hell.

A chugging prawn boat slides round Cuddy Point
Where in a gale
I spread my batwing jacket and jumped farther
Than I've jumped since. There's where I used to sail
Boats looped from rushes. On the jetty there
I caught eels, cut their heads off and watched them slew
Slow through the water. Ah - Cape Finisterre
I called that point, to show how much I knew.

While Hamish sketches, a crofter tells me that
The Scalpay folk,

Though very intelligent, are not Spinozas . . .
We walk the Out End road (no need to invoke
That troublemaker, Memory, she's everywhere)
To Laggandoan, greeted all the way -
My city eyeballs prickle; it's hard to bear
With such affection and such gaiety.

Scalpay revisited? - more than Scalpay. I
Have no defence,
For half my thought and half my blood is Scalpay,
Against that pure, hardheaded innocence
That shows love without shame, weeps without shame,
Whose every thought is hospitality -
Edinburgh, Edinburgh, you're dark years away.

Scuttering snowflakes riddling the hard wind
Are almost spent
When we reach Johann's house. She fills the doorway,
Sixty years of size and astonishment,
Then laughs and cries and laughs, as she always did
And will (Easy glum, easy glow, a friend would say) . . .
Scones, oatcakes, herrings from under a bubbling lid.
Then she comes with us to put us on our way.

Hugging my arm in her stronger one, she says,
Fancy me
Walking this road beside my darling Norman!
And what is there to say? . . . We look back and see
Her monumental against the flying sky
And I am filled with love and praise and shame
Knowing that I have been, and knowing why,
Diminished and enlarged. Are they the same?

SHIANT - SHEPHERDS

Shiant

Ian Stephen

a calm below teeming airspace.
a task for a flight controller:
steering the routes of razorbills,
puffins and ripple-breasting shag.

shored gear in fertiliser bags,
strung with one sheep, three dogs.
the dinghy does fine as a ferry:
men, beasts and bags to our taller hull.

a shared distinction in these five
who worked out a week on the Shiants;
on turf-padded rocks, mid Minches,
while their climber ewes had their lambs.

standard eccentricity in their hats,
like that Aran-knit of tweed-wool, but
these men with the calm in their bellies
lived somewhere obscured to ourselves.

DESERTED ISLAND

Anna Adams

Scarp

Since people left, corncrakes move in
to nest in deepening grass between locked houses.
I hear at night, each time I wake,
the creaking of the crake
like croaking frogs, or like a telephone
at the distant end of the line.
It calls and calls, again and then again;
yet is is not quite that desolate
repeated call, unanswered, in a house
which people have left forever, where people lie dead,
or are, and have been, all their lives,
both deaf and dead to urgent summonings.

The corncrake calls and calls; the double note
signalling other crakes.

I saw one, stepping, cautiously, through grass,
followed by what I thought at first were mice -
dark-mottled little crakes.

This rock may shrug its people off
but it is populous.
Withdrawing itself within a purdah of rain
the island pulls mist-curtains close.
Behind gauze veils we hear the giggling birds
and chattering of burns in dialect
as they run seaward, flowing over grass,
shouting like gutter-children mocking middle-class
intruders in their district.
Out in the rain, stepping across the burns,
I find the ground is mined with snipes.
Touched off, they panic up
to ricochet off nothing as they fly.

I lie awake. The corncrake calls all night.
Its voice, if it is a voice, saws like a file
working through prison bars.

A FANK: MEN COUNTING AND CLAIMING THE SHEEP IN SPRING

Scarp

Anna Adams

In a north-easter, by a white-toothed sea,
counting and being counted in a pen,
the humble grey beasts eddy round the knees
of humble perpendicular beasts, men.

Their dogs grin from the walltop; clipped ears bleed
as the new lambs are claimed: necessity
castrates the rams, doses, daubs blue or red
each bulging-eyed, exploited property.

These mutual slaves together in a fold
of tumbled stones, beside the snarling sea,
are wealth in its beginning, whence the world
gets riches, yet it looks like poverty.

SAILING BY

Anna Adams

Scarp

Half-past-midnight's music, 'Sailing By'
heralds the weather-warnings for trawlermen,
yachtsmen, tankers, lonely ocean-rowers
pondskating over unmapped water-dunes
in areas like Rockall, German Bight.
Then 'Coastal waters' traces a top-heavy chart
of squat, square-headed Britain, sitting hard
on Kent and Sussex, hatching the Isle of Wight,
bathing its Cornish feet in Atlantic suds
and hugging Wales to its narrow chest, while Ireland
swims away to the West.

I could chant a limited personal list
of seaside stations: Selsey Bill, Southend,
Felixstowe, Sutton-on-Sea, St. Margaret's Bay;
then Leiston, Filey, Swanage, Lulworth Cove -
to map my childhood summers.
War was hiatus. Bardsey, Lindisfarne,
then Inishmore, and Scarp in the Hebrides
where I first heard that music - 'Sailing By' -
as I enjoyed my late-night fireside bath
while southwest gales rocked house and boat and bay
and all the rest to sleep.

The Hebrides are twenty years away
but that unchanging half-past-midnight tune
still makes our long-abandoned sheiling rise
around me and enclose me, instantly.
Soft tilley-lamplight shows me wooden walls -
tongued and grooved - the painted vertical grain
rivering-upward, swerving round dead-wood eyes.

Our looted, or else beachcombed, bric-a-brac -
flat-irons, gannet-skulls, wild flowers in jars
crowd the shelf above the stove
backed by the pinned-up map of Scotland's rocks.

Juniper Horizontalis's rickety bones -
twisted by wind-sprawl on the dresser-top.
Above, on a shelf, four blue enamel plates
like portholes, and - of utilitarian beauty -
four thick white army-surplus porridge bowls.
In a drawer, my inherited tin of needles and thread,
scissors and suchlike, holds my mother's ghost -
imprisoned air of home - and on the walls
paintings of sea, and mountains in the sea,
and one of an ultramarine and scarlet lobster
such as my sons braved drowning for, most mornings.

The sisal matting filters white sea-sand,
not dust, and the dying fire would smell of peat,
not coal, if it hadn't gone out; and the stripe of light
beneath the bedroom door has gone out too
with a sigh from the pressure lamp, as 'Sailing By'
sailed by and arrived at silence.
The phantom house collapses along with the island,
sinking fathoms down in the foaming sea,
drowning my mother's old tin with her mending-gear
decades deep in the past. Unreachable, now,
is the coffined air that used to transport me home.

ST. KILDA

Neil Curry

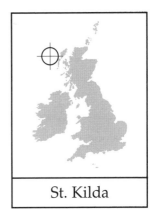

St. Kilda

I
The map the dominie* had tacked up
On the schoolroom wall didn't even show
St Kilda, but then only a foreigner
Would have needed one to find his way past Mull
And Skye, out through the Sound of Harris, then on
For fifty empty miles over the
Oily pitch and swell of the grey
North Atlantic.

       Any St Kildans,
Out of sight of land, with bad weather closing,
Knew they'd only to watch the flight-paths
Of the birds: guillemot and gannet would wreck them
On the stacs round Borreray, while puffins
Scuttering back wave-high to Dun
Would prove a safe guide home to Hirta
And the Village Bay.

II
Birds. Or angels even
They must have seemed, the women
Plucking, in a cloud of feathers
At the haul of fulmars their menfolk

Had themselves plucked off the cliffs
Of Conachair; cragsmen spidering,
Thirty fathoms down, along ledges
Of guano, dependent on sheer faith

In their neighbours and on a horsehair rope.
Claim life those cliffs could, but always would
Sustain it while there were sea-birds
In such thousands to stew or dry;

Even a gannet's neck, turned inside out,
Made a snug boot, and oil from the fulmar
Not only fuelled their lamps, but was a panacea
For no matter what ills or ailments of the island.

III

Ultima Thule it was
Until the Victorians discovered it,
Sending in their missionaries
To pound out the parable

Of the Prodigal Son
To people who hadn't
Anywhere to stray to
And had never seen a pig.

Then steamers came, and summer visitors
With gimcrack charities and new disease,
Tipping the cragsmen with a penny each
To see them capering about on Conachair;

Pennies that the winter ferryman
Would finger from the eyelids of their dead.

IV
By lantern-light
They loaded a few more
Sticks of furniture
And the last of the sheep,
And then they drowned their dogs.

In the morning,
According to custom,
In every empty house
There was a bible left
Open at Exodus.

* _Teacher_

ST. KILDA'S PARLIAMENT:
1879 - 1979 *(The photographer revisits his picture)*

Douglas Dunn

St. Kilda

On either side of a rock-paved lane,
Two files of men are standing barefooted,
Bearded, waistcoated, each with a tam-o'-shanter
On his head, and most with a set half-smile
That comes from their companionship with rock,
With soft mists, with rain, with roaring gales,
And from a diet of solan goose and eggs,
A diet of dulse and sloke and sea-tangle,
And ignorance of what a pig, a bee, a rat,
Or rabbit look like, although they remember
The three apples brought here by a traveller
Five years ago, and have discussed them since.
And there are several dogs doing nothing
Who seem contemptuous of my camera,
And a woman who might not believe it
If she were told of the populous mainland.
A man sits on a bank by the door of his house,
Staring out to sea and at a small craft
Bobbing there, the little boat that brought me here,
Whose carpentry was slowly shaped by waves,
By a history of these northern waters.
Wise men or simpletons - it is hard to tell -
But in that way they almost look alike
You also see how each is individual,
Proud of his shyness and of his small life
On this outcast of the Hebrides
With his eyes full of weather and seabirds,
Fish, and whatever morsel he grows here.
Clear, too, is manhood, and how each man looks
Secure in the love of a woman who
Also knows the wisdom of the sun rising,

Of weather in the eyes like landmarks.
Fifty years before depopulation -
Before the boats came at their own request
To ease them from their dying babies -
It was easy, even then, to imagine
St Kilda return to its naked self,
Its archaeology of hazelraw
And footprints stratified beneath the lichen.
See, how simple it all is, these toes
Playfully clutching the edge of a boulder.
It is a remote democracy, where men,
In manacles of place, outstare a sea
That rattes back its manacles of salt,
The moody jailer of the wild Atlantic.
    Traveller, tourist with your mind set on
Romantic Staffas and materials for
Winter conversations, if you should go there,
Landing at sunrise on its difficult shores,
On St. Kilda you will surely hear Gaelic
Spoken softly like a poetry of ghosts
By those who never were contorted by
Hierarchies of cuisine and literacy.
You need only look at the faces of these men
Standing there like everybody's ancestors,
This flick of time I shuttered on a face.
Look at their sly, assuring mockery.
They are aware of what we are up to
With our internal explorations, our
Designs of affluence and education.
They know us so well, and are not jealous,
Whose be-all and end-all was an eternal
Casual husbandry upon a toehold

Of Europe, which, when failing, was not their fault.
You can see they have already prophesied
A day when survivors look across the stern
Of a departing vessel for the last time
At their gannet-shrouded cliffs, and the farewells
Of the St. Kilda mouse and St. Kilda wren
As they fall into the texts of specialists,
Ornithological visitors at the prow
Of a sullenly managed boat from the future.
They pose for ever outside their parliament,
Looking at me , as if they have grown from
Affection scattered across my own eyes.
And it is because of this that I, who took
This photograph in a year of many events -
The Zulu massacres, Tchaikovsky's opera -
Return to tell you this, and that after
My many photographs of distressed cities,
My portraits of successive elegants,
Of the emaciated dead, the lost empires,
Exploded fleets, and of the writhing flesh
Of dead civilians and commercial copulations,
That after so much of that larger franchise
It is to this island that I return.
Here I whittle time, like a dry stick,
From sunrise to sunset, among the groans
And sighings of a tongue I cannot speak,
Outside a parliament, looking at them,
As they, too, must always look at me
Looking through my apparatus at them
Looking. Benevolent, or malign? But who,
At this late stage, could tell, or think it worth it?
For I was there, and am, and I forget.

LADY GRANGE ON ST. KILDA

Edwin Morgan

St. Kilda

The tide turns like a regiment for home and I am left
backstitching the day, brocading the sea for my bedspread.
In the kirkyard each unmarked stone has a different ring
so my people will know which one I'm singing in.

Tonight, the wind will come trampling the hair of the grass
dancing his twostep of profitless journeys, billowing his fist
in my face, throwing his conjuror's knives at my ear
whispering *Who, lady? Who do you think you are?*

But I shall buckle on my thistle shoes
and dance with my children the stones back out across
the blue sea holly. Then the rain will take me in her sail

to the nursery's utter west, where the moon is as pale
as a spoon, and the sun is the eye of a doll going down
and the bedcovers lift and sink with the lungs of the drowned.

*1732 - The Edinburgh judge Lord Grange, wishing to be rid of his wife,
had her taken away and abandoned on the remote island of St Kilda.*

HOME AGAIN

Siusaidh NicNeill

Lewis

Home again
to the flat island
to see the horizontal washing
flapping manically
the sharp northeasterly
springing pegs
from the line
and the smoke coughing
from the stack.
From the southwest
it would blow back
to choke the firesiders.

Translated from Gaelic by the Author

NO RETURN

Iain Crichton Smith

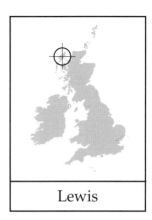

Lewis

No, really you can't go back to
that island any more. The people
are growing more and more unlike you
and the fairy stories
have gone down to the grave in peace.

The wells are dry now and the long grasses
parched by their mouths, and the horned cows
have gone away to another country
where someone else's imagination
is fed daily on milk.

There were, you remember, sunsets
against which the black crows were seen
and a moonlight of astonishing beauty
calmed at midnight by waters
which you're not able to hear.

The old story-telling people
have gone to their last houses
under the acres of a lost music.
These have all been sold now
to suave strangers with soft voices.

It is a great pity that your cottage
preserved in January by clear ice
and in June surrounded by daisies
has been sold to the same strangers
and the bent witches evicted.

If you were to return now the roofs
would appear lower, the walls would have no echoes,
the wavelike motion would be lost,
the attics where you read all day
would be crammed with antiques.

No, you cannot return to an island
expecting that the dances will be unchanged,
that the currency won't have altered,
that the mountains blue in the evening
will always remain so.

You can't dip your mouth in the pure spring
ever again or ever again be haunted
by the "eternal sound of the ocean".
Even the boats which you once rowed
have set off for elsewhere.

The witches wizards harlequins jesters
have packed up their furniture and guitars.
The witches have gone home on their broomsticks
and the conjurors with their small horses
and tiny carts have departed

leaving the island bare, bleak and windy,
itself alone in its barren corner
composed of real rocks and real flowers
indifferent to the rumours and the stories
stony, persistent.

LEWIS IN SUMMER

Derick Thomson

Lewis

The atmosphere clear and transparent
as though the veil had been rent
and the Creator were sitting in full view of His People
eating potatoes and herring,
with no man to whom He can say grace.
Probably there's no other sky in the world
that makes it so easy for people
to look in on eternity;
you don't need philosophy
where you can make do with binoculars.

Translated from Gaelic by the Author

THE BIER

Derick Thomson

Lewis

Arnish light on my right,
Muirneag cloaked,
a coverlet on the Barvas Hills,
a shroud on Hol,
we grasp the bier-poles,
rocking and plunging on the surface of memory.

Translated from Gaelic by the Author

WHEN THE DARK COMES

Derick Thomson

Lewis

When the dark comes
over you, taking Muirneag away
and Bayble Hill and Hol,
when your sheep are lying,
the grass dark in the womb of night,
the new moon not yet up,
I shall throw this handful of peats on the fire
and it will make some light.

Translated from Gaelic by the Author

THE GAELIC LONG TUNES

Les Murray

Outer Hebrides

On Sabbath days, on circuit days,
the Free Church assembled from boats and gigs
and between sermons they would tauten
and, exercising all they allowed of art,
haul on the long lines of the Psalms.

The seated precentor, touching text,
would start alone, lifting up his whale-long tune
and at the right quaver, the rest set sail
after him, swaying, through eerie and lorn.
No unison of breaths-in gapped their sound.

In disdain of all theatrics, they raised
straight ahead, from plank rows, their beatless God-paean,
their giving like enduring. And in rise
and undulation, in Earth-conquest mourned
as loss, all tragedy drowned, and that weird
music impelled them, singing, like solar wind.

OLD BOAT

Ian Stephen

Pabaill Island

We touched the transom
and could not see
Pabaill island.

There was no wind.
The stern was still.
The boat, shored,

lay calm in flaked
paint; the wood sores
bared to haar.

Too cold to sleep,
we floated dry
miles from noise.

DEAD FIRES

George Mackay Brown

Hoy

At Burnmouth the door hangs from a broken hinge
And the fire is out.

The windows of Shore empty sockets
And the hearth coldness.

At Bunertoon the small drains are choked.
Thrushes sing in the chimney.

Stars shine through the roofbeams of Scar.
No flame is needed
To warm ghost and nettle and rat.

Greenhill is sunk in a new bog.
No bending woman
Blows russet wind through squares of ancient turf.

The Moss is a tumble of stones.
That one black stone
Is the stone where the hearth fire was rooted.

In Crawnest the sunken hearth
Lit many a story-tranced mouth,
Old seamen from the clippers with silken beards.

The three-toed pot at the wall of Park
Is lost to woman's cunning.
A slow fire of rust eats the cold iron.

The sheep drift through Reumin all winter.
Sheep and snow
Blanch fleetingly the black stone.

From that good stone the children of the valley
Drifted lovewards
And out of labour to the lettered kirkyard stone.

The fire beat like a heart in each house
From the first cornerstone
Till they led through a sagged lintel the last old one.

The poor and the good fires are all quenched.
Now, cold angel, keep the valley
From the bedlam and cinders of A Black Pentecost.

KIRKYARD

George Mackay Brown

Orkney Isles

A silent conquering army,
The island dead,
Column on column, each with a stone banner
Raised over his head.

A green wave full of fish
Drifted far
In wavering westering ebb-drawn shoals beyond
Sinker or star.

A labyrinth of celled
And waxen pain.
Yet I come to the honeycomb often, to sip the finished
Fragrance of men.

LAMBHOLM

Pauline Stainer

Orkney Isles

Here
at the salt edge of things,
the six-cornered snowflake
falls on simple moss.

Madonna of the Nissen huts -
your candles spit
before the creatures
of bread and wine

the sea reassembles its engines,
Italian prisoners of war
build the barriers
in a wolfish light

their prayers
tiny depressions
in the silence
like fossil raindrops.

ROBERT LOUIS STEVENSON DREAMS OF ORKNEY IN SAMOA

Orkney Isles

Pauline Stainer

Last night
a wind came over the sea,
keen as a swan's bone,
particular with the dead.

I saw my father
and grandfather, inspecting
the major lighthouses
as the skerries smoked by.

Here, azure orchids burn,
kingfishers refract
the great white light -
but for a moment

I weigh the examined life,
the necessary exile,
against the way light behaves
between the islands.

CHILDHOOD

Edwin Muir

Wyre

Long time he lay upon the sunny hill,
  To his father's house below securely bound.
Far off the silent, changing sound was still,
  With the black islands lying thick around.

He saw each separate height, each vaguer hue,
  Where the massed islands rolled in mist away,
And though all ran together in his view
  He knew that unseen straits between them lay.

Often he wondered what new shores were there.
  In thought he saw the still light on the sand,
The shallow water clear in tranquil air,
  And walked through it in joy from strand to strand.

Over the sound a ship so slow would pass
  That in the black hill's gloom it seemed to lie.
The evening sound was smooth like sunken glass,
  And time seemed finished ere the ship passed by.

Grey tiny rocks slept round him where he lay,
  Moveless as they, more still as evening came,
The grasses threw straight shadows far away,
  And from the house his mother called his name.

THE ORKNEYS

Peter Fallon

North Ronaldsay

Be all that as it may,
on a fertile isle
north of here - called Ronaldsay -
short-tailed sheep, their fleeces
shades of red, tan and grey,

have matched their need
between the tides
to newfound feed.
They've salvaged from the rocky shore
a fill of seaweed.

Foragers, since the crofters mured
them outside the fields
they conserved for crops. Inured
to it - 'one hand washes
the other' - they've endured.

They've been learning not to care
for ages now,
on scanty fare.
They must slake their thirsts on dew
and other alms of the air.

RENOIR IN ORKNEY

Stewart Conn

Orkney Isles

Monet might have made himself at home
among these flat, green islands
like giant water-lilies. Cezanne even,
with cliff-faces all cones and cylinders.

Not that my vision is impaired -
more a narrowing of the spectrum
to a harmony of glistening silk
as if too much light were being let in,

but without the embracing warmth
to which I am accustomed: seascape
and skyscape, a constant radiance.
It would need the skin of the place

to burst a blood vessel, or myself
to stab at it with a palette knife:
then there'd be something I could express.
Only this morning the world disappeared;

the boat I was in surrounded
by quicksilver, the bordering land
erased in mist. Like a composer
frantic for some variation

beyond a single high-pitched note
sustained in his brain,
I crave a cacophony of colour,
before my mind disintegrates.

At least with the fishermen
I am at home. Their tanned features
merit the mixing of pigments:
my yellows and reds are in business again.

As for the womenfolk, baiting the line
has made their fingers like my own
and worse: knife-gashes to the bone . . .
Nudes are out. For one thing, their

Kirk concedes no such tradition.
For another, contemplate the climate.
But something in me burns. I must
start again. I have found a girl

with skin like mother-of-pearl;
am working on still lives of lobsters;
and will distribute at the solstice
canvases of wild flowers, like mottled flame.

FAIR ISLE PATTERN

James Rankin

Fair Isle

Here I sit in this quiet place
My needles noisy as gulls that
Flash and speak and bring me a
Kind of peace.

I am old, old growing back at
My only pace. These wools. The smell
Of Fair Isle when I was a girl;
The blue oarsman who took me in his boat.

I sit and wait. And now they come.
The colours come. The needles speak.
My fingers spawn fish boy and girl;
The flowers spin and turn deep in the weave

Of years, each coloured wool a child.
I count them in my sleep, Aaron and Michael
Joanne and Drew white faces that
Seem to live and breathe.

So many garments. So many children.
The heart's a blur and will not leave
The intricate pattern I from
These wools conceive.
The fire is dying. The effort stops
The needles still. My tired arms sleep,
The garment is complete.

It is growing dark. My tongue's a peat.
Now all the colour's one. In my larder
The gulls hack at my small store.
The sea is at my door.

I FOUND

Fair Isle

Fair Isle Primary School.

On Sompal, I found
A starfish, rough like gravel,
And a jellyfish.
It holds a bad secret.
It stings you and sizzles your hand.

In Hjukni Geo, I found
Mermaids' purses.
Yellow ones with curly ends
Like the twisty tendrils of beans,
Black ones shaped like stretchers.
Hold them hard and they crunch like a crisp.

Down Finniquoy, I found
A sheep's skull.
Its jaw was shaped like a shoe,
And the eyes stared at me, bold and round.

At the Nirth Haven beach, I found
Limpets, purple inside,
A shell like frozen waves.

At Haswells, by Sheep Rock, I found
Metal, sharpened on cliff ends.
It flakes, it crumbles.
It flakes, it crumbles.
It's tangled like a rope.
It could spear a selkie or a sheep's feet.

At Steensi Geo, I found
Oil.
It spreads from one animal to another
Like electricity.
When one cable breaks
The lights go off.

Written with the help of Katrina Porteous

SEASONS ON FOULA

Leona Gear (aged 7)

Foula

At Christmas
The snow was too deep on Soberlie
And the sheep were buried.

The sea came bashing against Gaada Stack
Crash! Slash! Bang!

The Sneug had snow on the top
Like white clouds.

In April
Our sheep had their lambs at Gravins.
I had a caddy lamb.
I called her Sparky.
Instead of watching TV
I would make her a bottle of milk.

In May
The tirricks at the airstrip
Made a squawking sound.

Out by the banks in July
There were beautiful flowers, pink and red.

Down by the loch swans glided slowly,
Orange beaks and yellow beaks.

At Boulder Beach
I sat alone on the rocks.
The sea sparkled like crystals and diamonds.
Killers whales dived.
Their backs made half-circles in the sea.

On Hamnafield
I collected heather berries, shiny and tasty.
An allen came down from the sky
And thumped my head.

In September
We had cruiis.
Lots of people and lots of dogs
And lots of shouting!
Clip, clip, clip with the shears.

In October
The silver leaves in the fields turned golden brown.
The hills went dark.

Penny's horses came in off the hills.

There was more night than day.

caddy lamb	-	pet lamb
tirricks	-	terns
allen	-	Artic skua
cruiis	-	sheep round-ups

Written with the help of Katrina Porteous.

In 1996, Leona was the only pupil attending Foula Primary School.

FOULA, AULD YULE, 6th JANUARY

Katrina Porteous

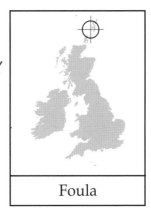

Foula

Shut the door and pass the bottle
Round the circle of light.
One by one let us drink to the days
The sun makes ripe,

And join in your riddle, Aggie Jean, in the ring
Of the stove's peat reek,
While, long past midnight, the child in my lap is falling
Into sleep;

Into widening circles of sleep, that will carry her
Who knows where.
Let us drink to the fire within. We know too well
The dark out there.

Foula folk still celebrate Christmas on January, 6th and New Year on January, 13th in accord with the old Julian calendar.

FOULA, NEW YEAR, 13th JANUARY

Foula

Katrina Porteous

Hamnafield and the Sneug lie untouched
By sun or breeze.
Ice grips the memory of last spring stone still.
Only the geese

Drift by the Mill Loch, soundless,
Spent as snow,
While the black fires of January hold their breath
Below.

Go, wild geese: fly south and tell him
How silence speaks;
How, in the clench of winter,
Summer sleeps.

SHETLAND 1973

John Betjeman

Fetlar, Yell, Foula

Fetlar is waiting. At its little quay
Green seaweed stirs and ripples on the swell.
The lone sham castle looks across at Yell,
And from the mainland hilltops you can see
Over to westward, glimmering distantly,
The cliffs of Foula as the clouds dispel.
Clear air, wide skies, crunch underfoot of shell -
The Viking kingdom waits what is to be.

Loud over Lerwick, seabirds wail and squawk,
Portent of Shetland's fast approaching foes -
The briefcased oilmen with their wily talk;
Soon we shall see, ranged all along the voes
Their hard-faced wives in ranch-type bungalows.

THE CAPTAIN

Kathleen Jamie

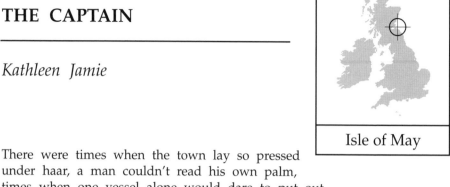

Isle of May

There were times when the town lay so pressed
under haar, a man couldn't read his own palm,
times when one vessel alone would dare to put out
from the harbour's crooked arm
to the mist-thickened bay. There, he'd shut down
the engine, and lean out over the rail,
closing his eyes. So we'd drift, until,
at the edge of his sense, of this world,
came the faint mewl of kittiwakes
and whummeling gulls , and so dead
slow or dead slow, he'd nudge past the cliffs,
judging the distance to hold this,
his small boat of the living, by those cries,
you could almost believe were of souls.

ROOTS

Peter Mortimer

Lindisfarne

In the Manor House Garden
a new cabbage,
arisen.
Contemplated by St. Aidan,
salted by the sea,
shadowed by the Priory.
It shares the wind
that wastes the castle,
shares the island's clenched survival,
clinging tight to fragile roots.

HAIKU FROM HOLY ISLAND

Peter Mortimer

Lindisfarne

The granite church
crumbling. The breaking waves
still breaking.

*

To Cuthbert's Island
the longest
journey.

INITIAL ILLUMINATION

Tony Harrison

Lindisfarne

Farne cormorants with catches in their beaks
shower fishscale confetti on the shining sea.
The first bright weather here for many weeks
for my Sunday G-Day train bound for Dundee,
off to St. Andrew's to record a reading,
doubtful, in these dark days, what poems can do,
and watching the mists round Lindisfarne receding
my doubt extends to Dark Age Good Book too.
Eadfrith the Saxon scribe/illuminator
incorporated cormorants I'm seeing fly
round the same island thirteen centuries later
into the *In principio's* initial I.
Billfrith's begemmed and jewelled boards got looted
by raiders gung-ho for booty and berserk,
the sort of soldiery that's still recruited
to do today's dictators' dirty work,
but the initials in St. John and in St. Mark
graced wth local cormorants in ages,
we of a darker still keep calling Dark,
survive in those illuminated pages.
The word of God so beautifully scripted
by Eadfrith and Billfrith the anchorite
Pentagon conners have once again conscripted
to gloss the cross on the precision sight.
Candlepower, steady hand, gold leaf, a brush
were all that Eadfrith had to beautify
the word of God much bandied by George Bush
whose word illuminated midnight sky
and confused the Baghdad cock who was betrayed
by bombs into believing day was dawning
and crowed his heart out at the deadly raid
and didn't live to greet the proper morning.

Now with noonday headlights in Kuwait
and the burial of the blackened in Baghdad
let them remember, all those who celebrate,
that their good news is someone else's bad
or the light will never dawn on poor Mankind.
Is it open-armed at all that Victory V,
that insular initial intertwined
with slack-necked cormorants from black lacquered sea,
with trumpets bulled and bellicose and blowing
for what men claim as victories in their wars,
with the fire-hailing cock and all those crowing
who don't yet smell the dunghill at their claws?

PRAISE THE LORD AND PASS THE AMMUNITION

Valerie Laws

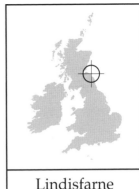

Lindisfarne

The rainbow arch hangs in space
at Lindisfarne, a cannonball's leap
frozen in stone. Hail and rain rattle
the walls like shot, the sea keeps up
its cavalry charge. Cows graze
salt-bleached grass, descendants
of those spared by the monks
who spent more on gunpowder
than parchment.

Cold as steel, the salty air
that cramped their fingers
as they hefted the sacks
of black meal, protection
against the devil's reivers.

Within, by the fire, Eadfrith
lit the pages of the gospels,
on calf-skin pricked with needles,
tatooed with inks. So slow a fuse
burning in red and gold, his truth
needing a little help from the gunsmith,
shielding the spark, so easily flaring up
and catching hold.

Black meal: flour paid as protection money on Northumbria/
Scotland border, giving us the word blackmail.

ON ST. CUTHBERT'S ISLAND

Andrew Waterhouse

St. Cuthbert's Island

A nervous scramble over wracks
to this small acre of dolerite
and scurvy grass to crouch together
out of the wind and under the cross,

where his invisible enemies
may have been defeated by fasting
and prayer and we clutch at each other
as a mist comes in with a useless

new moon and the village lights
appear and fade and the sleet
starts and our faces are numbed,
which is what finally forces us

to give in and carry his love and devils
and hunger back to the mainland.

(for Stella)

SIGNS

Joan Hewitt

St. Mary's Island

Three hundred million years ago, this island
was nudging the equator, and took off
northwards on a whim, to shudder down
in rifts and seams in this cold sea.

Twenty-four years ago, the first signs
that you wanted to be out, a tightening
in the back, and the feeling that I had to be
near water, this was where we came.

Today I sit much further out
on the blunt grey folds of rocks
which drowse like ancient elephants
under rugs of bright-green algae;

I'm remembering how heavily I trod
in my black cape around the lighthouse,
telling myself that if one bird
were perched on that obelisk in the sea

you and I and the birth would be just fine.
So what was I to make of three -
the cormorants - cramped in that narrow space,
no room to spread their wings?

(for Laura; and Anna and Kate)

SAILING DIRECTIONS IN FOG

Alan Gay

Farne Islands

When fog creeps-in, rather than risk The Callers
(rocks sent to torment the tides and make topaz blooms
rise from the seabed) leave them to their watery trade;
to strike terror into the hearts of longship marauders
and founder the Forfar: all but five.

Best stand-off!

If you must try for land, go through Wideopen Scars
fixing Oxcars in line with Seahouses pier end.
Hold Bamburgh Castle close to Inner Farne cliffs,
Holy Island Old Law Beacon, east of Megstone.

As the fog follows you in
swing into the Kettle with all sails standing,
luffing-up on the snub of your anchor chain
close under St. Cuthberts Chapel.

Now ... listen across the Staple Sound
for Longstone's *Mooon! - Mooon!*
to harmonise moans of hauled-up seals,
in counterpoint to the alarms of gulls and terns

that raise such a cacophony you cannot hear yourself speak.

And nor would you wish to.

FLYING THROUGH RADAR

Alan Gay

Farne Islands

Shadows pick a jagged course through Longstone's rocks.
A trawler bashes south.
Echelons of scarlet flashed puffins on tramlines
fly headlong for sunset burrows.

Trapped in the rays of the trawler's radar as it sweeps the island
the birds lose all sense of direction,

become heartbeat blips across a green-lit- screen.

The rays mangle their wings
into rags that flap madly
in a stunned-tumble
to the sea's furnace.

Once past, momentum locks their flight back
onto its true course.

The sun still melts.
The rocks still turn black and hell-red.

AN ABSENCE OF ISLANDS

Norman Nicholson

Look west
from Cumberland,
east from the North Sea shore,
where the wind is a spume of tossed terns and fulmars
of fumes with smothering feathers of soot;
look beyond seaweed and sewage,
pebbles and quick-sand and the oiled ebb channel -
and always,
at the far rim of the sea's grooved disk,
whatever the direction, whatever the slide of tide,
in an absence of islands
the horizon seems the same.

THE ISLAND

Kevin Crossley-Holland

Seven days, seven nights in a place of stone:
Atlantic anvil where winds and water hone
Men to what they are, long bundles of bone.

Seven days, seven nights in a place of stone
Where each man learns he is at last alone,
So quickly comes to love, forgive, condone.

Seven days, seven nights in a place of stone.
Saffron flowers in the fissures are soon grown
To all they can become: each one its own

Spirit's song, momentary wild laughter thrown
Against grey walls, the grey sky, the grey sea.

ISLANDMEN

R. S. Thomas

And they come sailing
From the island through the flocks
Of the sea with the boat full
Of their own flocks, brimming fleeces
And whelk eyes, with the bleating
Sea-birds and the tide races
Snarling. And the dark hull bites
At the water, crunching it
To small glass, as the men chew
Their tobacco, cleaning their mind
On wind, trusting the horizon's
Logic.

These are the crusted men
Of the sea, measuring time
By tide-fall, knowing the changeless
Seasons, the lasting honeysuckle
Of the sea. They are lean and hard
And alert, and while our subjects
Increase, burdening us
With their detail, these keep to the one
Fact of the sea, its pitilessness, its beauty.

MORE ISLANDS

Eiléan Ni Chuillenáin

A child afraid of islands, their dry
Moonlit shoulders, sees in a deep gutter
A stone, a knot in the stream.
She feels the gasping of wrecks,
Cormorants and lighthouses.

She grows up to detest airports
But feels the sea in the waves of her hair
And icebergs in a storm of lemonade.

She knows there are some islands the sea avoids.
Boats leaving the coastline are led far astray
By strong currents, long mackerel shoals.
High on their dark rocks a man
Shouting for help, a bell ringing
Can call over hundreds of high tides
And not be heard, raising no echo
Until an injured seagull blown flat along the stones
Touches the hard earth, or the first fire
Lit by a castaway cuts the darkness
Liberating silence.

THE ISLAND

Derrick Thompson

When we reached the island
it was evening
and we were at peace,
the sun lying down
under the sea's quilt
and the dream beginning anew.

But in the morning
we tossed the cover aside
and in that white light
saw a loch in the island,
and an island in the loch,
and we recognised
that the dream had moved away from us again.

The stepping-stones are chancy
to the second island,
the stone totters
that guard the berries,
the rowan withers,
we have lost now the scent of the honeysuckle.

Translated from Gaelic by the Author

THE TRAVELLER HAS REGRETS

G. S. Fraser

The traveller has regrets
For the receding shore
That with its many nets
Has caught, not to restore,
The white lights in the bay,
The blue lights on the hill,
Though night with many stars
May travel with him still,
But night has nought to say,
Only a colour and shape
Changing like cloth shaking,
A dancer with a cape
Whose dance is heart-breaking,
Night with its many stars
Can warn travellers
There's only time to kill
And nothing much to say:
But the blue lights on the hill,
The white lights in the bay
Told us the meal was laid
And that the bed was made
And that we could not stay.

THE ISLAND

Iain Crichton Smith

"And as for that island," so he said,
"we shall remember it always however we change,
the sun on the lochs on a clear day.
We shall not comb our hair without remembering
the windy grass on the moor."

ISLAND

R.S. Thomas

I would still go there
if only to await
the once-in-a-lifetime
opening of truth's flower;

if only to escape
such bought freedom, and live,
prisoner of the keyless sea,
on the mind's bread and water.

THE POETS

Anna Adams was born in 1936 and educated at Harrow and Hornsey Schools of Art. She has had five collections of verse published by Peterloo Poets. Her *Selected and New Poems: A Green Resistance* was published by Enitharmon in 1996. She is currently working on a long verse-letter to a dead poet.

John Betjeman (1906 -84) was born in Highgate and educated at Marlborough and Magdalen College, Oxford. His verse autobiography, *Summoned by Bells* appeared in 1960. He was appointed Poet Laureate in 1972. He edited and wrote a number of Shell Guides. His *Collected Poems* achieved enormous popularity and is frequently reprinted.

Brian Biddle has been writing poetry since his retirement from a career in scientific research and lecturing and is interested in bridging the gap between science and the arts. His poems have been published in a number of magazines and he is Treasurer of Toddington Poetry Society.

Angela Blacklock-Brown was born and raised in Dumfries and Galloway. Formerly a teacher, she now combines part-time work in the Scottish Poetry Library with writing. She has travelled the world and has had poems published in magazines and anthologies and has won a short story competition about sailing.

Eavan Boland was born in 1944 in Dublin but spent part of her childhood in London. She read Latin and English at Trinity College, Dublin. Her *Collected Poems* was published in 1995. Her prose work entitled *Object Lessons* is a reflection on women, poetry and the Irish literary temperament. She has been a professor of English at Stamford University, California.

Alix Brown is a therapist working with damaged adolescents. She lives in Shropshire with her partner and an assortment of animals. Both she and her partner spend a lot of time in Scotland and both are members of the Iona Community.

George Mackay Brown (1921-96) was born and brought up in Orkney. He was persuaded by his fellow Orcadian poet, Edwin Muir to attend Newbattle Abbey College, near Edinburgh where Muir was the principal. He went on to study at Edinburgh University and did postgraduate study on the poetry of Gerard Manley Hopkins. He returned to Orkney and rarely left these islands again. His *Selected Poems* was published by John Murray.

George Bruce (1909 - 2002) was born in the fishing port of Fraserburgh, in north-east Scotland. The sights and sounds of the fishing community reverberate in his first collection, *Sea Talk* (1944). His collection, *Pursuit: Poems 1986-98* won the 1999 Saltire Book of the Year Award. In his 90th year, he remarked that he was just getting into his stride.

Paddy Bushe is the author of six collections of poems in English and Irish, the most recent being *The Nitpicking of Cranes* (Dedalus, 2004). He has also published a number of translations. He lives in County Kerry.

Myles Campbell was born in the Isle of Skye and writes primarily in Scottish Gaelic. He has published five collections of verse, the latest *Saoghal Ur* (New World) from Diehard Press, Calender, 2003. A bilingual selection of his verse appears in an Anthology of 20th Century Gaelic Verse, Edited by Ronald. I.M. Black (Polygon, 1999) He was crowned Bard at the Royal National Mod, Largs, in 2002.

Robert Cortean Carswell was born in 1950 and was privileged to study the Manx Gaelic language with the late Douglas Fargher. He was also inspired by the late Mona Douglas.

Eithne Cavanagh loves islands and hopes to visit many more around Ireland and Scotland. Her poems which have won prizes have been published in magazines worldwide. Her first collection, *Bone and Petals,* appeared in 2001. She teaches creative writing in Dublin.

Eiléan Ni Chuillenáin was born in Cork City in 1942. She has won the Patrick Kavanagh Award and the O'Shaughnessy Award of the Irish-American Cultural Institute. She has published seven collections of verse. She is a Fellow of Trinity College, Dublin. She is married to Macdara Woods and they have a son, Niall.

Stewart Conn was born in Glasgow and grew up in Ayrshire but now lives in Edinburgh. He was for many years a producer in the BBC's Radio Drama Department. His collections include *Stolen Light: Selected Poems* (Bloodaxe, 1999) and his latest collection, *Ghosts at Cockcrow* (Bloodaxe, 2005) includes many poems written during his three years as Edinburgh's first Poet Laureate.

David Constantine was born in Salford in1944. He is a fellow in German at The Queens College, Oxford. His collection, *Watching for Dolphins* appeared in 1983 and his *Selected Poems* in 1991. His *Collected Poems* was published by Bloodaxe in 2004. He has also translated the *Selected Poems of Friedrich Holderlin (1996).*

Kevin Crossley-Holland was born in Buckinghamshire in 1941 and educated at Bryanston School and St. Edmund Hall, Oxford. He now lives in North Norfolk. He has written numerous books for children and is a reteller of traditional tales and a translator of Anglo-Saxon. His *Selected Poems* was published by Enitharmon in 2001.

Neil Curry was born in Newcastle-upon-Tyne in 1937 and now lives in the Lake District. He read English at Bristol University and taught in Canada and England. His collections include *Ships in Bottles* (Enitharmon, 1988) and a sequence inspired by his 500 mile journey along the Pilgrim Road to Santiago de Compostyela, *Walking to Santiago,* (Enitharmon, 1992).

Douglas Dunn was born in Renfrewshire in 1942. After graduating from the University of Hull, he worked under Philip Larkin in the Brynmor Jones Library. He is now professor of English at St.Andrews University. He has published many collections of verse, including the moving *Elegies* which was written after the death of his first wife from cancer (Faber,1985). He is the editor of the Faber Book of Twentieth Century Scottish Verse (1992).

Peter Fallon lives with his family on a small farm in County Meath, Ireland where he is editor and publisher of The Gallery Press. His recent books include *News of the World: Selected and New Poems* and *The Georgics of Virgil,* the Poetry Book Society Recommended Translation.

G.S. Fraser (1925-80) was born in Glasgow and studied at St. Andrews University. He served in the Middle East during World War 2 and then worked as a journalist and was an influential literary critic. He published many volumes of poems and his *Collected Poems* was published by Leicester University Press.

Robin Ford is a native of the Isle of Wight and started writing at the age of 56 with the Green Room Poets after a severe bout of mental illness from which he has suffered throughout his life. He has published a poem sequence entitled, *After The Wound* and a collection entitled *Never Quite Prepared For Light* with Arrowhead Press.

Alan Gay has anchored his yacht in many of the islands in this anthology which have inspired his poetry. Although born in England, he now lives in Scotland and writes full-time, navigating the deeper reaches of poetry. His recently published pamphlet, *Songs of Sorrow* and some of his other poems can be read by emailing Alancharlesgay@aol.com and linking to his website.

Leona Gear is now fifteen years of age and still lives on Foula with her crofter parents. She is a pupil in the secondary school at Lerwick where she stays in the school hostel. On Foula, she breeds Shetland ponies and hopes to be a vet. She no longer writes poems but enjoys writing short stories.

Valerie Gillies, poet and teacher, was reared in Southern Scotland and studied in Mysore, South India. She is currently Fellow in Creative Writing at the University of Edinburgh. Her most recent books are *Men and Beasts,* (Luath, 2000) and *The Lightening Tree,* (Polygon, 2002).

Roddy Gorman was born in Dublin in 1960 but he now lives on the Isle of Skye. He was Writing Fellow at the Gaelic college on Skye and has held other such appointments. His collections of verse include *Fax and other poems* which was published by Polygon in 1906.

W.S. Graham (1918-86) was born in Greenock. He worked as an engineer on Clydeside as a young man. He later settled in Cornwall whose landscapes and seascapes colour his poetry. His collection *The Night Fishing* (1955) uses the extended metaphor of a herring fishing expedition. His *Collected Poems* 1942-1977 was published by Faber in 1979.

Jane Griffiths was born in Exeter in 1970. After reading English at Oxford, she worked as a bookbinder in London and Norfolk. She returned to Oxford and completed a doctorate on the Tudor poet, John Skelton. Her first collection, *A Grip on Thin Air* was published by Bloodaxe in 2000.

Gerard Hanberry is a teacher of English and a musician. He lives on the shores of Galway Bay. He was shortlisted for a Hennessy award in 2000. His first collection of poems entitled *Rough Night* was published by Stonebridge Publications in 2002.

Tony Harrison was born in Leeds in 1937. *His Selected Poems* was first published by Penguin in 1984. His collection, *The Gaze Of The Gorgon* was published by Bloodaxe in 1992 and was awarded the Whitbread Prize for Poetry. He is Britain's leading theatre and film poet and *The Shadow Of Hiroshima and other film poems* was published by Faber in 1995 and awarded the William Heinemann Prize in 1996.

Kay Hathway is a social worker with a lifelong love of poetry. She started a poetry writing group in 1995 as a way of getting feedback from her work. This group meets monthly in her large garden shed and has around fifteen members. She has had poems published in competition anthologies.

Seamus Heaney born in 1939 was educated at St. Columb's College, Derry and Queen's University, Belfast. In 1972, he moved to the Republic of Ireland. His early poetry is deeply rooted in the farmland of his youth. His later poetry explores the use of words in wider social and political contexts. He was awarded the Nobel Prize for Literature in 1995. His *Collected Poems 1966-96* was published by Faber in 1999.

Joan Hewitt lives with her German partner in Tynemouth, occasionally dipping into the freezing North Sea and trying to finish a first poetry collection. Poems published in London Magazine and Mslexia. Awards in international competitions, 2003 Ledbury, (2nd) 2004 Mslexia (2nd), 2005 Kent and Sussex (3rd).

David Hodges is a monk on Caldey Island, off Tenby, Pembrokeshire. Published widely in periodicals and anthologies, his books: *Songs from Solitude, On the Night Tide* and *Delayed by Rough Seas* can be obtained from Caldey Abbey or its website.

Molly Holden was born in Wiltshire and later moved to Worcestershire. She developed multiple sclerosis and died tragically young. In a poem anticipating her death, she wrote that she hopes that her ashes will fall 'among the fine grass of home.' Her *New and Selected Poems* (Carcanet) are out of print.

Kathleen Jamie was born in 1962 in Renfrewshire. Her first full collection was entitled *The Way We Live* (1987). Her travel books include *The Golden Peak* (1992) which describes her travels in northern Pakistan. She now teaches creative writing at St.Andrews University. *Mr.& Mrs Scotland Are Dead: Poems 1980-1994* was published by Bloodaxe in 2002.

Valerie Laws has a degree in mathematics and theoretical physics. She was involved in a project entitled Quantum Sheep in which words of haiku were written on the backs of living sheep. She edited an anthology of Star Trek poems for IRON Press. Her first full collection, *Moonbathing* was published by Peterloo in 2003.

Michael Longley was born in Belfast in 1939 and educated at Trinity College, Dublin. He is one of the triumvirate of important Ulster poets who emerged in the 1960s, along with Seamus Heaney and Derek Mahon. He is married to the literary critic, Edna Longley. His *Selected Poems* is published by Faber.

Thomas Lynch is a poet, essayist and funeral director in the small town of Milford in Michigan. His wonderful collection of essays entitled *The Undertaking - Life Studies from the Dismal Trade* is a modern classic. His best known collection of poems is entitled *Still Life In Milford*.

Norman MacCaig (1910-96) was born and educated in Edinburgh. He was a primary schoolmaster for many years. Many of his poems were inspired by the landscapes of the north-west Highlands and the Outer Hebrides. He published many collections of verse and edited two anthologies of Scottish poetry. The revised and expanded edition of his *Collected Poems* was published in 1993.

Hugh MacDiarmid (1892-78) was born in Langholm in the Scottish Borders. He was a founder of the Scottish National Party in 1928. He and his wife spent a number of years on the Shetland Isle of Walsay. His great poem written in synthetic Scots, *A Drunk Man Looks at the Thistle* appeared in 1926. His autobiography, *Lucky Poet* contains moving passages about his life on Walsay.

Sorley MacLean (1911-96) was born on the island of Raasay and educated on the Isle of Skye and at the University of Edinburgh. He was headmaster of Plockton High School for many years, He is regarded as one of the finest Gaelic poets of the 20th century. *From Wood to Ridge: Collected Poems in Gaelic and English* was published in 1989.

Donald A. MacNeill (1924-95) was born in the Hebridean island of Oransay and he later became a farmer on the neighbouring island of Colonsay. He was a musician and singer and many of his Gaelic poems were intended to be sung, sometimes to a traditional Gaelic air.

Derek Mahon was born in Belfast in 1941 and studied at Trinity College, Dublin and the Sorbonne. He has held journalistic and academic appointments in London and New York. A member of Aosdana, he has received numerous awards including the Irish Academy of Letters Award and the Scott Moncrieff translation prize.

Edwin Morgan was born in 1920 and was educated in Glasgow and was appointed a professor of English at the same university in 1975. His *Glasgow Sonnets* (1972) vividly evoke the urban landscape he loves. He has translated many poets into English, including Neruda and Mayakovsky. His *Collected Poems* is published by Carcanet.

Peter Mortimer is a poet and playwright who lives in the Northumbrian coastal village of Cullercoats. He is the editor of IRON Press and artistic director of Cloud Nine Theatre Co. His latest book from Mainstream, *Cool for Qat, a Yemeni Journey 1930-2004* is due Summer 2005. Due from Five Leaves Press is *Off the Wall - The Journey of a Play*.

Edwin Muir (1887-59) was born on the main island of Orkney but moved to the tiny island of Wyre when he was an infant. *An Autobiography* movingly depicts his island childhood and his family's move to Glasgow where his parents and his two brothers died within five years. He and his wife, Willa translated Franz Kafka into English. His *Collected Poems* was published by Faber.

Richard Murphy was born in County Mayo in 1927 and spent five of his childhood years in Ceylon before being educated in Ireland and England. He bought High Island and lived alone there for a number of years. He later gave the island away and it is now a bird sanctuary. His *Collected Poems* was published by Gallery Press in 2000.

Les Murray was born in 1938 in New South Wales. He spent his childhood and adolescence on his grandfather's dairy farm. He lived with his wife and children in England and Europe before returning to Sidney to pursue a career as a full-time writer. In his poetry, he strives to appeal to a broad readership, not just to a coterie of intellectuals. His *Selected Poems* is published by Carcanet.

Norman Nicholson (1914-87) was born in the iron town of Millom in Cumberland where he lived all his life, apart from his teenage years in a tuberculosis sanatorium. This experience influenced much of his poetry which is rooted in his own loved area. His *Collected Poems* was published by Faber.

Suisiddh NicNeil lived on the Isle of Lewis for many years and now lives on the Isle of Skye where she works in Gaelic education. She writes in English because she thinks her Gaelic isn't good enough.

Julie O' Callaghan was born in Chicago in 1954 but now lives in Dublin. She is a widely anthologised poet for children. Her collection, *Edible Anecdotes* (Dolmen Press,1983) was a Poetry Book Society Recommendation and her collection, *What's What* (Bloodaxe, 1991) was a Poetry Book Society Choice.

Michael O' Siadhail was formerly professor at the Dublin Institute for Advanced Studies. His collection, *The Gossamer Wall* was the result of many years' immersion in the testimonies of survivors of the Holocaust. In his poem, *The Face*, he writes of 'A promise to remember, a promise of never again.'

Katrina Porteous was born in Aberdeen and now lives in Northumberland. She was Writer-in-Residence to Shetland Arts Trust in 1996-97. Her books include *The Lost Music (Bloodaxe 1996), The Wund an' the Wetter (IRON Press 1999)* and *The Bonny Fisher Lad (People's History 2003).*

Alan Pryce-Jones was a poet, critic and the editor of a number of anthologies.

Kathleen Raine (1908-2003) was the daughter of a Scottish mother and a Northumbrian father. She was educated at Girton College, Cambridge. Much of her poetry is inspired by the landscapes of the Highlands and Islands of Scotland where she experienced a sense of the sacred. Her *Collected Poems* appeared in 1981. She wrote three volumes of autobiography.

James Rankin was formerly Fellow of Creative Writing at the University of Dundee.

Alistair Reid was born in Galloway in 1926. He graduated from St. Andrews University after war service in the navy. *Oases* (Canongate, 1997) is a collection of prose and poetry. *On the Blue Shores of Silence* (Harper/Collins, 2004) is a translation of his friend, Pablo Neruda's poems of the sea.

Iain Crichton Smith (1928-98) was born in Glasgow but moved to the Isle of Lewis when he was two. He lived with his crofter grandmother in the village of Babel. He studied at Aberdeen University and became a teacher and taught for a number of years at Oban High School. His Lewis childhood, dominated by the rigid doctrines of the Free Church, haunts his poems. His *Collected Poems* was published by Carcanet.

Pauline Stainer was born in 1941 and educated at St. Anne's College, Oxford and Southampton University. She lived for a time in the Orkney Isles and her collection *Parable Island* contains a number of intense lyrics about the islands. *The Lady & the Hare: New and Selected Poems* was published by Bloodaxe in 2003.

Iain Stephen was born in the Outer Hebrides in 1955. He has had poetry published in many countries. His first collection entitled *Malin, Hebrides, Minches* was published by Dangaroo Press. He has also had collections published by Polygon and Morning Star. He has held a Robert Louis Stevenson residency and has gained a Creative Scotland Award.

R.S. Thomas (1913-2000) was born in Cardiff and educated at St.Michael's College, Llandaff and University College, Bangor. He was ordained as a priest in the Church of Wales in 1936. He spent many years working in remote hill parishes, preaching to tiny congregations and this experience colours his many volumes of verse. His *Collected Poems* was published by Orion in 2000 and his *Collected Later Poems 1988-2000* was published by Bloodaxe in 2004.

Derick Thomson was born in 1921 in the Isle of Lewis. He is a former Professor of Celtic at Glasgow University. He is the author of many books, including *An Introduction to Gaelic Poetry (1974)* and *The Companion to Gaelic Scotland (1983).* He has published seven collections of poetry, including *Plundering the Harp (1982).*

Andrew Waterhouse was born in 1958 in Lincolnshire. He was a farm worker before studying environmental studies at university. He lived in rural Northumberland where he worked as teacher and a freelance writer. His collection *In* won the Forward Prize for Best First Collection in 2000. He took his own life in 2001.

James Knox Whittet *(contributor and the book's editor)* was born and brought up in the Hebridean island of Islay, and went on to read English at Cambridge University. His first collection is entitled *A Brief History of Devotion* (Hawthorn Press, 2003) and his collaboration with the Norfolk artist, John Richter is entitled *Seven Poems For Engraved Fishermen* (2004). He won the 2004 Crabbe Memorial Poetry Competition. He is collaborating with the photographer Sue Anderson on a book about Islay.

ACKNOWLEDGEMENTS

Anna Adams *Deserted Island* and *A Fank: Men Counting and Claiming the Sheep in Spring* from Island Chapters, reprinted by permission from Arc Publications. *Sailing By* from Flying Underwater (2004) published by Peterloo Poets, reprinted by permission of poet.

John Betjeman *Shetland 1973* from Collected Poems, reprinted by permission of John Murray (Publishers).

Brian Biddle *Wild Paeony* reprinted by permission of poet.

Angela Blacklock- Brown *Night Landing Canna* reprinted by permission of poet.

Eavan Boland *The Achill Woman* from Selected Poems, reprinted by permission of Carcanet.

Alix Brown *Iona Dance* from This is the Day, edited by Neil Paynter, 2002 reprinted by permission of Wild Goose Publications.

George Mackay Brown *Dead Fires* and *Kirkyard* from Selected Poems, reprinted by permission of John Murray (Publishers).

George Bruce *The Stones of Iona and Columba* from Collected Poems, reprinted by permission of Polygon.

Paddy Bushe *Sceilg Monks* by permission of poet.

Myles Campbell *The Buzzard* by permission of poet.

Robert Cortean Carswell *The Sound of Morning* by permission of poet.

Eithne Cavanagh *Saltee Island* first appeared on Electric Acorn; *Inishbofin Sheep Shearing* from Bone and Petals published by Swan Press and *Tory Island Images* first appeared in The Connaught Telegraph, 2 Jan. 2002, all reprinted by permission of poet.

Eiléan Ni Chuillenáin *More Islands* from The Second Voyage (1986) reprinted by kind permission of the author and the The Gallery Press, Loughcrew, Oldcastle, County Meath, Ireland.

Stewart Conn *Sabbath, North Uist* and *Renoir in Orkney* from Selected Poems published by Bloodaxe Books, reprinted by permission of poet.

David Constantine *Islands* from Collected Poems, reprinted by permission of Bloodaxe Books.

Kevin Crossley-Holland *The First Island* and *The Island* from Selected Poems (2001) published by Enitharmon, reprinted by permission of poet.

Neil Curry *St. Kilda* reprinted by permission of Enitharmon.

Douglas Dunn *St. Kilda's Parliament* from St. Kilda's Parliament published by Faber & Faber, reprinted by permission of poet.

Peter Fallon *The Blaskets* and *The Orkneys* by permission of poet.

Fair Isle Primary School *I Found* from Lights of Islands edited by Sergio Mariotti reprinted by permission of Fair Isle Primary School.

Robin Ford *Island* by permission of poet.

Alan Gay *Sailing Directions in Fog* and Flying *Through Radar* by permission of poet.

Leona Gear *Seasons on Foula* by permission of poet.

Valerie Gillies *The Old Woman's Reel* from The Chanter's Tune published by Canongate Books Ltd., reprinted by permission of poet.

Roddy Gorman *Gaelic* reprinted by permission of Polygon.

Jane Griffiths *Island* from A Grip on the Air published by Bloodaxe Books 2000, reprinted by permission of Bloodaxe Books.

Tony Harrison *Initial Illumination* from Gaze of the Gorgon, published by Bloodaxe Books 1992, reprinted by permission of poet.

Kay Hathway *Ramsay Island Makeover* and *Holy Island*, by permission of poet.

Seamus Heaney *Lovers on Aran* from Selected Poems reprinted by permission of Faber & Faber.

Joan Hewitt A version of *Signs* first published in Under Your Skin, 2003, an anthology of Newcastle University's Creative Writing MA. Reprinted by permission of poet.

David Hodges *Caldey Island* reprinted by permission of poet.

Kathleen Jamie *A Dream of the Dalai Lama on Skye* from Mr & Mrs Scotland are Dead: Poems 1980-1984 published by Bloodaxe Books 2002, reprinted by permission of Bloodaxe Books. *The Captain* by permission of poet.

Valerie Laws *Praise the Lord and Pass the Ammunition* by permission of poet.

Michael Longley *Leaving Inishmore* from Selected Poems published by The Random House Group, reprinted by permission of The Random House Group.

Thomas Lynch *Argyle's Return to the Holy Island* from Still Life in Milford published by The Random House Group, reprinted by permission of The Random House Group.

Norman MacCaig *Below the Clisham, Isle of Harris; After Many Years* and *Return to Scalpay* from Collected Poems published by Polygon, reprinted by permission of Polygon, an imprint of Birlinn Ltd.

Hugh MacDiarmid *Perfect* from Collected Poems published by Carcanet, reprinted by permission of Carcanet.

Sorley MacLean *Hallaig* from Hallaig in Nua-Bhardachd Ghaidhlig Modern Scottish Gaelic Poems A Bilingual Anthology introduced by Donald MacAulay, published by Canongate Books Ltd., reprinted by permission of Canongate Books.

Donald A MacNeill *A Fisherman* from Moch Is Anmoch published by House of Lochar 1998, reprinted by permission of House of Lochar.

Derek Mahon *Rathlin* from Collected Poems (1999) reprinted by kind permission of the author and the Gallery Press, Loughcrew, Oldcastle, County Meath, Ireland.

Edwin Morgan *An Arran Death* and *Lady Grange on St. Kilda* from Collected Poems published by Carcanet, reprinted by permission of Carcanet.

Peter Mortimer *Roots* and *Haiku from Holy Island* from 100 Days on Holy Island published by Mainstream Publishers 2002, reprinted by permission of poet.

Edwin Muir *Childhood* from Collected Poems published by Faber & Faber, reprinted by permission of Faber & Faber.

Richard Murphy *High Island, Walking on Sunday* and *Tony White at Inishbofin* from Collected Poems (2000) published by The Gallery Press, reprinted by kind permission of the author and The Gallery Press, Loughcrew, Oldcastle, County Meath, Ireland.

Les Murray *The Gaelic Long Tunes* from Selected Poems published by Carcanet, reprinted by permission of Carcanet.

Suisiddh NicNeil *Home Again* by permission of poet.

Julie O'Callaghan *The Great Blasket Island* from What's What published by Bloodaxe Books (1991) reprinted by permission of Bloodaxe Books.

Michael O'Siadhail *Islander* from Our Double Time published by Bloodaxe Books (1998) reprinted by permission of Bloodaxe Books.

Katrina Porteous *Foula, Auld Yule 6th January* and *Foula, New Year 13th January* by permission of poet.

Iain Crichton Smith *Island Poems, At the Firth of Lorne, No Return* and *The Island* from Collected Poems published by Carcanet, reprinted by permission of Carcanet.

Pauline Stainer *Lambholm* and *Robert Louis Stevenson Dreams of Orkney in Samoa* from The Lady & The Hare; New & Selected Poems, published by Bloodaxe Books 2002, reprinted by permission of Bloodaxe Books.

Ian Stephen *Shiant-Shepherds* and *Old Boat* from Malin, Hebrides, Minches, published by Dangaroo Press,1983, reprinted by permission of poet.

R.S. Thomas *That Place* and *Island* from Collected Later Poems 1988-200 published by Bloodaxe Books, reprinted by permission of Bloodaxe Books. *Islandmen* from Collected Poems published by JM Dent, a division of The Orion Publishing Group Ltd., reprinted by permission of The Orion Publishing Group Ltd.

Derick Thomson *Lewis in Summer, The Bier, When the Dark Comes* and *The Island* from Collected Poems, reprinted by permission of poet.

Andrew Waterhouse *On St. Cuthbert's Island* from Good News from a Small Island published by Midnag Arts Group 2001, reprinted by permission of the poet's estate.

James Knox Whittet *Moving with the Times* from A Brief History of Devotion published by Hawthorne Press 2003 and *Island Wedding*, reprinted by permission of poet.

Every effort has been made to trace copyright holders, but in some cases this has not been possible. The publishers would be grateful to hear from any copyright holders not here acknowledged.

INDEX